German Immigrants, American Pioneers

THE BRUNNERS OF SCHIFFERSTADT

Patricia Ogden
Boyce Rensberger

BLUE MUSTANG
P R E S S
Blue Mustang Press
Boston, Massachusetts

ISBN: 978-1-935199-24-3
PUBLISHED BY BLUE MUSTANG PRESS
www.bluemustangpress.com
Mansfield, Massachusetts

Printed in the United States of America

German Immigrants, American Pioneers

THE BRUNNERS OF SCHIFFERSTADT

Patricia Ogden
Boyce Rensberger

Written with the generous cooperation of the
Frederick County Landmarks Foundation.

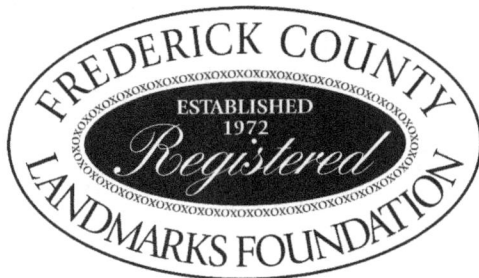

FREDERICK COUNTY
ESTABLISHED
1972
Registered
LANDMARKS FOUNDATION

For Avery as well as Sofia, Niko, Dean and Maeve.
As we dwell in the past,
all of you are our hopes for the future.

CONTENTS

Acknowledgements

Patricia Ogden began her work on this book some six years ago, doggedly mining libraries and archives in Maryland and Pennsylvania. In that time, she has come to owe a debt of gratitude to many who have been sources of facts, interpretation and moral support through her long project.

It was Melanie Gettier who first suggested that Ogden's pocket full of notes on the history of the house and the Brunner family could one day become a book. Bernie Callan shared his wealth of knowledge of Schifferstadt and Frederick history. The late Pat Miller was an early mentor and friend. Reiner Prochaska provided translations of German text and explanations of German culture. Elizabeth Covington was a great editor and proofreader. And Pam Cederloff was a constant source of support and encouragement.

Ogden's family—Melissa and Mike as well as Carrie and Patrick—were always interested and supportive as mom delved into yet another area of interest. Gratitude also goes to her extended family for their continued interest and encouragement. Closer to home, husband Rick patiently endured hours of research, trips to historic sites and time tapping away on a keyboard. His help in keeping the walls from falling in and his never-failing support made the pursuit of this avocation possible.

Boyce Rensberger joined the project late in its gestation and is grateful for all the time, dedication and brainpower that Patricia has brought to bear. She is grateful for his ability to find a story in a stack of research papers and his masterful writing skills, which have elevated this project to a level far beyond the original concept.

Together, we had much assistance from several good people. Bruce Bomberger shared his knowledge of 18th century farming. Mary Mannix and Carolyn Magura at the Maryland Room were instrumental in the success of the research project. Others read chapters and corrected errors: Carrie Albee, Tom Hornyak, Joe Lubozynsky and Irwin Richman. Irvin Molotsky copy edited the text. Walter "Butch" Chalkley of Blue Mustang Press tirelessly formatted everything for printing. Errors that remain—and no doubt there are some—are the authors' fault. But given the technology of "printing on demand," it should be possible to correct them quickly in later printings. We invite notification of mistakes through the book's website at *brunnerbook.info*.

Lastly, we express our deep gratitude to the Frederick County Landmarks Foundation, which owns and manages the Schifferstadt Architectural Museum. Their efforts over nearly half a century have given us an outstanding window to the early American past in Maryland. Administrator Tiffany Ahalt and her predecessor, Melanie Gettier, were helpful in many ways. Ogden and Rensberger are volunteers with the Foundation and are pleased to have spent many hours in the old house, absorbing something of its history and sharing it all with visitors.

Introduction

A surprisingly complete story of the founding and settlement of Frederick County, Maryland, can be told through the pioneering Brunner family and their Maryland house, which they called Schifferstadt after their home town in the old country. We know many details of the story's beginning in the 1700s as the Brunners prepared to escape their ravaged German homeland. And in the 21st century we have the evidence of how they lived in Maryland—the stone house that stands today as an architectural museum in the City of Frederick.

The house says so much about the Germans who settled in America that in 2017 the U.S. Department of the Interior awarded it the elite designation as a National Historic Landmark, only the second site to be so honored in Frederick County. For one thing, it had a typically German clean, energy-efficient, radiant heating system.

In this book we have tried to tell as much of the overall story as can be documented by historical records of the family and of the times in which they lived. We have relied upon the work of historians and of contemporaneous observers who left us accounts of what they saw. And we have combed through government and church records of the Pennsylvania and Maryland colonies, which yielded surprising points of interest.

We learned, for example, that one of the Brunners didn't turn in as many crows' heads as the law required and that another was convicted of breaking the Sabbath. We tell those anecdotes, but the greater story we discovered was the ambition and perseverance of the German immigrants who came to colonial America and helped build this country.

This book is a collection of several different ways of telling the story. There is straight narrative history. But there are also collections of anecdotes based on legal documents and even what we call a fictionalized "Year at Schifferstadt." That chapter is meant as a kind of "living history" of life at Schifferstadt but in words rather than costumes. And we include an account of people who owned the house through the centuries, including an epic battle of more than 40 years when one stubborn owner "sold" the place to somebody else but refused to sign the deed to make the transaction legal. And finally, we look at the house as it stands today, a room-by-room tour in words and pictures. We hope that readers who wish to delve further into the specifics will find the references section at the back helpful. Nearly all our facts and figures, marked by superscript numbers, are drawn from publicly available documents, including some easily accessible online.

As students of American history know well, the spelling of names was rendered variously over the years. Here we reproduce the different versions from the records and leave it to readers to understand that, for example, Stephen Remsberger is the same man as Stephen Ramsburg or any of several other versions that show up here. But if we found an authoritative source, such as the church record of the marriage of Joseph and Cathrina Brunner, we stuck with that spelling throughout.

More broadly, our story is about the German heritage of Frederick County. In the early days, German immigrants, often poor and often consigned to labor as indentured servants, were feared and resented by established British settlers, even by the liberal-minded Benjamin Franklin. In time, however, they were admired for their work ethic as well as their successful farms and shops. German immigrants thrived and soon came to play important civic roles in their adopted homeland. Today more Americans can trace at least part of their ancestry to Germany than to any other country.

This is the story of that heritage, told through the vehicle of one pioneering immigrant family that rose from impoverished servitude to a comfortable well-being and even a degree of prosperity.

1

A Horrific Homeland

At the age of 50, Joseph Brunner and his wife, Cathrina, two years younger, should have been enjoying the fullness of lives well lived. Yes, they had buried two children, but that was not unusual in their day some 300 years ago. After all, they had six surviving children, two of them already married and having given the Brunners the joys of being grandparents.

But life in Klein Schifferstadt, their village in what is today southwestern Germany, was not good. Wars had devastated the region for decades. Crop failures and bad weather had led to outright famine for some. The economy was in shambles. A bleak future lay ahead for the whole Brunner clan.

Joseph and Cathrina led a large extended family. Still living at home were Maria Cathrina, 19, Johannes, 18, Henderick, 13, and six-year-old Elias. Nearby lived their eldest son Jacob, his wife Maria Barbara and their two children. Joseph and Cathrina's daughter Anna Barbara, married to Christian Getzendanner, and their two children likely also lived close by.[1]

All fourteen of them would become pioneer families in Frederick County, Maryland, some even playing prominent roles in the area's civic and military life. But in the early 1700s, they had looked at life in Germany and could foresee only the same, unrelenting miseries.

The causes of the family's distress were widespread in the German-speaking principalities of 18th century Europe and would lead tens of thousands of Germans to uproot themselves from their ancestral homelands and embark on a dangerous migration to a place nearly 4,000 miles away, a place none of them had ever seen and about which they had only heard vague stories of uncertain credibility.

Indeed, Europe was in the grip of one of the worst climatic, economic and political catastrophes it would suffer until the World Wars centuries

1

later. The exodus of Germans, most from the same region in the upper (southern) reaches of the north-flowing Rhine River, called the Palatinate or Rhine Pfalz, would become one of the great mass migrations of human beings. By the 21st century, some 50 million Americans would be able to trace their ancestry to Germany—the largest group in the United States sharing the same national origin. The Pennsylvania Dutch (originally Deutsch, or Deitch, in the local German dialect), remain a notable group. Maryland claims a similar, though smaller, German heritage.

Until the troubles began in the Palatinate, ancestors of the Brunners were living in a region of fertile valleys and beautiful scenery once considered "the garden of Germany"[2] if not of all Europe. But the Rhine valley's very attractiveness made it a tempting prize for various regional powers, starting as far back as the ancient Romans seeking to expand their empire. In later centuries French and German armies battled for possession. Then closer to the Brunners' time, in the mid-1600s, came the devastating Thirty Years' War between various Catholic and Protestant powers, one side seeking religious freedom as the other sought to stamp out heresy.

Fighting raged through many of the 224 separate German-speaking principalities, some officially Catholic, others officially Lutheran, but nowhere more frequently than in the Palatinate. So deeply was Catholicism embedded in some places that the local bishop was also the government ruler—the prince. The wars eventually killed an estimated eight million people in central Europe,[3] an estimated 25 percent to 40 percent reduction in population.[4] Once-thriving farms and fields were laid waste. Devastated economies left the survivors so demoralized, historians say, that it would take many years for them to recover.[5]

Not long after those wars had died down, Joseph Brunner was born in 1678 and baptized into the Reformed Church, a Protestant sect.[6] When Joseph was just 10 years old, war returned. The French under their brutal emperor, Louis XIV, invaded, pillaging whole towns and eventually killing an estimated 100,000 Germans. The French invasion brought devastation perhaps worse than that of the Thirty Years' War. If young Joseph did not personally witness the atrocities, he surely heard adults talking about them.

According to Henri Martin, a French historian, the emperor's secretary of state for war, the Marquis de Louvois, ordered numerous cities and

**The Palatinate
of the Rhine**
During the time of
the great Palatine
emigration to America.

villages in the Palatinate sacked and burned. When the marquis heard that Mannheim had not been obliterated, he ordered the city burned and "that not one stone should be left on another." Even the town of Speyer, just five miles from the Brunners' village of Klein Schifferstadt, was "condemned to the flames."[7] ("Klein," meaning small in German, was part of the name of the mostly Protestant village of perhaps 15 families to distinguish it from the bigger town across the Speyrbach River. That municipality, called Gross Schifferstadt, was largely Catholic.)[8]

So devastated were the Rhine Valley peoples that some began emigrating, heading to other parts of Europe and to Britain. The first contingent of Palatines, as they were called, emigrated to America in 1683. London saw the arrival of several thousand Palatines in 1709.[9] Most were Protestants escaping persecution by Catholic rulers. These included Lutherans and members of the German Reformed Church. These two groups would predominate among the first immigrants to Pennsylvania.[10]

Other non-Catholic groups that would eventually join the great migration across the Atlantic included several Anabaptist faiths, which rejected the infant baptism of Catholics, Lutherans and German Reformeds. The Anabaptists included the Mennonites, Amish and German Baptists (also called Dunkers).

The Brunners belonged to the German Reformed Church, in which Joseph served as an elder.[11] That sect eventually gave rise to today's United Church of Christ. Their village of Klein Schifferstadt was in the principality of Speyer, which was governed by a Catholic bishop who was also the ruling prince. As in much of Europe, church and state were not separate. The prince-bishop ruled as a feudal lord, the people of his realm vassals under him.

Joseph occupied a precarious position. He held a post (we don't know what sort) in the prince-bishop's court, surely dealing only with civil matters.[12] This suggests that he could read and write. But he was not a wealthy man. In fact, he was a vassal, legally bound to the prince-bishop who was the feudal lord. In addition, Joseph occupied a position of some status as an elder in the local Reformed Church. These are clues that he was literate. We have no evidence that he or his family were persecuted for religious reasons. No doubt, though, that the Brunners saw the arrows of persecution flying around them. And they

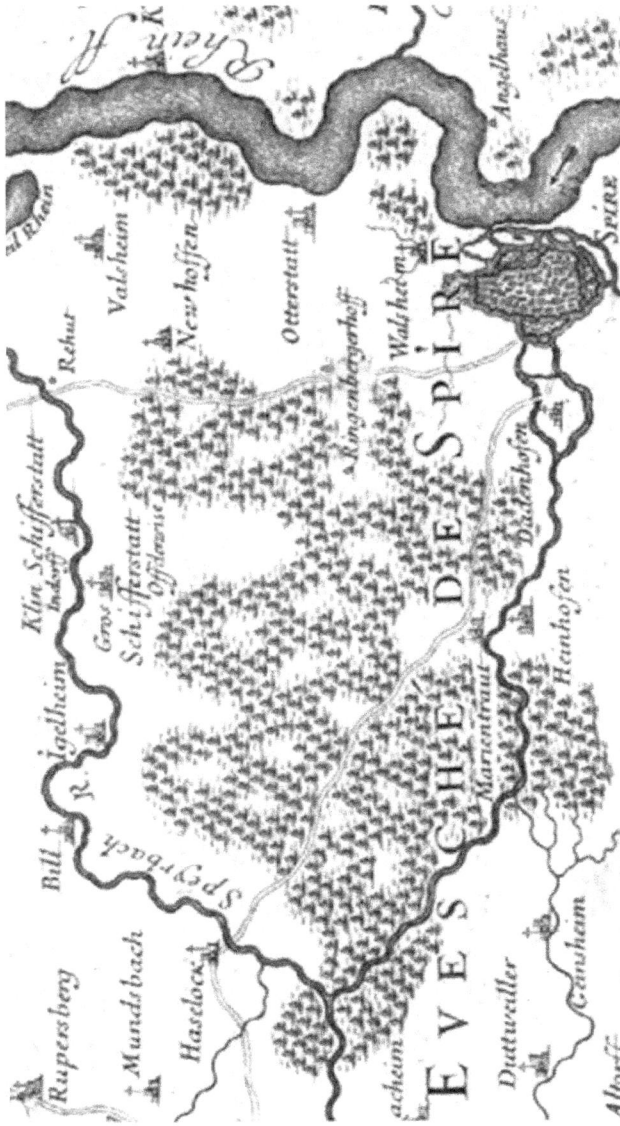

A detail from a 1695 French map of the Palatinate region. It shows the two Schifferstadts at the top, separated by the Speyrbach River. The town of Speyer, here spelled the French way, is at the lower right, on the Rhine River.

would have been acutely aware of the rigid class system that blocked ordinary people like them from improving their lot.

War and religious strife were not the only troubles in the region. Europe was experiencing what climatologists now call the Little Ice Age. In its worst years navigable rivers froze over each winter, the ice persisting well into the spring. Wine and allegedly even spirits froze. Fruit trees were killed.[13] Temperatures were too cool for some crops, and the growing season was too short for others.[14]

Chaotic weather during the early 1700s brought other miseries. In 1725, for example, the summer was so wet that fungal blight destroyed many grain crops. The next year was so hot and dry in Germany that grain in the field was infested by a different fungus, causing what growers call rust. Rye, one of the chief crops in the Rhinepfalz, became contaminated by an unusually poisonous fungus called ergot.[15] Eating tainted rye can cause severe, sometimes fatal illness in humans and livestock. Ergot poisoning became widespread in the area, causing people to behave bizarrely, sometimes leading others to accuse them of demonic possession.[16]

To make matters worse, many prince-bishops began to emulate the lavish lifestyle of Louis XIV, his ways having been made known when France conquered parts of the German lands. To pay for their extravagances, the prince-bishops imposed ever steeper taxes on their people.[17]

The question, ultimately, is not why the Brunners would decide to leave but why anyone would choose to stay.

2

A New Frontier Beckons

Meanwhile, thousands of miles away from Europe, Britain's American colonies were doing well enough, but their colonial rulers weren't making as much money from their lands as they had expected. The king had made William Penn the owner of Pennsylvania. Maryland went to Lord Baltimore, a title passed from George Calvert to his descendants. The idea was that these men, called proprietors, would sell or rent their vast lands and rake in the money.

The proprietors' problem was that English settlers and their descendants were building cities and plantations along the seacoast—Boston, New York, Philadelphia, Baltimore, Annapolis and on south to Charleston. Their economy depended heavily on trade with the Old World, so they needed to be near seaports.[1] The proprietary possessions stretched far inland, into the western wilderness, lands sometimes occupied by various Indian tribes and sometimes claimed by Britain's arch-nemesis, France. So, like land speculators to this day, the proprietors advertised farther afield for rent-paying tenants.

Penn had a bright idea. He was aware of the many troubles in German-speaking Europe and he believed Germans to be sober minded and hard working. After all, they had once made the Rhine valley into lush and productive farmland. Could not these people do the same for the Pennsylvania interior? And, he believed that Germans would serve as a buffer between the coastal English and the risky hinterlands.[2]

In the 1670s and 1680s Penn, a Quaker and a fluent German speaker, personally made several trips to the Rhinepfalz, talking up the opportunities in his colony. He had pamphlets and even books printed in German and circulated among Palatine towns and villages.[3] Word of the alleged opportunities in America doubtless reached Klein Schifferstadt. But the Brunners did not immediately take the leap.

William Penn

Perhaps they had heard that there were unscrupulous sales agents roaming Europe, talking up a supposedly idyllic life in America, some literally saying that gold could be found in the streets and that cows could graze on perfect pasturage all year round. Such claims were spread by men paid by ship captains to deliver human cargo for a trip across the Atlantic.[4] Many desperate Germans, Gottlieb Mittelberger wrote in his diary, were persuaded to emigrate by people who came to be called new-landers.

"These men-thieves," Mittelberger wrote, "inveigle people of every rank and profession, among them many soldiers, scholars, artists and mechanics. They rob the princes and lords of their subjects and take them to Rotterdam or Amsterdam to be sold there."[5] Those cities were ports for ocean-going ships.

Perhaps suspicious of the new-landers, the Brunners waited until 1728 when Joseph was 49 and even then took only the limited step of sending their eldest son, Jacob and his family. It may have been a testing of the distant waters, or perhaps Jacob, then 25 years old, was the most adventurous. In any case, we do find his name among the passengers who arrived in Philadelphia on August 23, 1728 aboard a ship called the *Mortonhouse*. He, his wife and their children were among approximately 200 passengers. Traveling with them was his sister, Maria Barbara, who had married Jacob Sturm, and their children.[6]

Like most German immigrants, the party from Schifferstadt arrived in Philadelphia, then the largest city in America and the main seaport. No record of Jacob's subsequent actions has come to light. But since the rest of the family made the journey the following year, Jacob's report must have been encouraging. Perhaps he was able to travel into the countryside and confirm that the area was already inhabited by large numbers of German farmers working rich soil. Jacob may have written to his parents that the land was fertile, the weather favorable and, perhaps just as encouraging, they all would be right at home with their German language, German foods and German customs.

The cathedral town of Speyer, the name being an archaic term for spires. The name may resonate with the people of Frederick, Maryland, which refers to its own "clustered spires."

3

Not So Fast

We do not know all the specifics of the Brunner family's journey to America, but we do know some surprising details. In the broader elements, the journey cannot have been much different from that of the thousands of other Palatine peoples who made the trip.

Before leaving their home in Klein Schifferstadt, the Brunners would have packed their most valuable possessions into a few trunks and sold everything else. They knew it was almost certain they would never return. But the family could not simply pick up and leave. Before emigrating, they would need manumission papers from the feudal prince-bishop, and they would have to pay to get them. To get permission to emigrate, Joseph had to declare the value of his assets and pay a hefty share to the ruler. Records in Germany show that on April 26, 1729, Joseph declared assets of 422 florins and after paying, had 292 florins left. Although old records give these figures, there is no good way to determine how the values compare to today's dollars. (A longer explanation of the monetary situation is in the end notes.)[1] But the numbers do show that it was a heavy tax amounting to about 30 percent of the family's total assets.

The Brunners then hired wagons to transport three generations overland about five miles to the larger town of Speyer, on the bank of the Rhine, the same town devastated years earlier by French armies. The party included Christian Getzendanner who was married to Anna Barbara, one of the Brunner daughters.[2] In Speyer the emigrants had another expense—buying passage on a boat heading downstream to the North Sea port of Rotterdam in the Netherlands. That alone was no easy trip, typically taking four to six weeks to cover 330 miles. The chief cause of delay was the fact that the

Rhine passed through some 36 separate German principalities, each with a customs house that had to be cleared.[3] Clearing meant paying a toll.[4] Another expense.

In bustling Rotterdam, surely the largest city the Brunners had ever seen, the typical German emigrant could spend several weeks waiting for a ship to take them on the next and worst part of the journey. They had to find food and lodging as they waited. Yet another expense.[5] Many Palatine refugees went broke by the time they reached Rotterdam.

The Rhine River from Schifferstadt to Rotterdam.

If a new-lander delivered immigrants to a ship captain, he would be paid for the effort. If the emigrant, like most, lacked money to pay for passage, the ship captain would expect to "sell" the person to some wealthy person in America—typically a merchant, a manufacturer or a prosperous farmer.

The price the captain collected would reimburse him for the cost of passage and, of course, yield a profit.[6]

On arrival such an immigrant became an indentured servant, obliged to work for anywhere from two to seven years to redeem the sum their new master had paid the ship captain. Such people were called redemptioners. Skilled tradesmen such as tanners, wheelwrights and weavers, being more valuable, might work as few as two or three years. Common laborers would be held longer.[7] For many years the government of Pennsylvania encouraged its wealthier citizens to purchase immigrants by granting the citizen 50 acres for each person brought into the country.[8] The great migration that established the largest share of today's American families was a business born of misery and, given the huge numbers seeking a better life, a profitable enterprise for a select few.

Setting sail out of Rotterdam ships carried anywhere from 150 to 400 passengers—men, women and children crammed below decks into what many would later describe as wretched conditions.[9] The first port of call was in England at a customs house, sometimes in Deal on the English mainland and sometimes in Cowes on the Isle of Wight, just off England's south coast. The east coast of America was, after all, English and the English authorities required vessels heading to America to check in at a customs house on the home islands. The trip to England alone took two to four weeks depending on the weather. Then a week or two could pass for ships to get into the busy English port, pass customs and sometimes wait for good weather to resume the journey.[10]

Then began the voyage to Philadelphia. The Brunner family, having secured passage on a ship called the *Allen,* settled in for what the adults must have known could be a dangerous trip. Depending on the season and the weather, it might take as little as six or eight weeks or in bad weather several more months.[11] We have no record of what the Brunners experienced. What was their food like? Did they have enough to last the journey? Did they suffer serious illness? Perhaps Jacob had warned his parents that the trip could be arduous, even dangerous, but ultimately worthwhile. For a great many who were determined to face the hazards, the experience was fatal.

Food was a major source of complaint. "Compared to most contemporary diets on shore, [the meals] were simply atrocious," the historian Klaus Wust wrote after reviewing numerous first-person accounts. "A ship's fare consisted mainly of items that would keep reasonably well for months such as hardtack, flour, peas, beans, rice, preserved meats and aged cheese. If the provisions taken aboard were fresh and securely stored, and the trip was uneventful, a healthy passenger could subsist on such a fare though its lack of balance and its heavy salt content made even strong individuals susceptible to a variety of illnesses. Moreover, seasickness, especially during the first days of the voyage, prevented many passengers from eating regularly while supplies were still fresh. After two or three weeks at sea, water turned increasingly putrid, beer became sour, and grain products humid and alive with vermin." If the trip was longer than expected, Wust added, there was "a real threat of starvation."[12]

To avoid famine, passengers sometimes caught mice and rats, said to be numerous on the ships. Casper Wistar, a passenger on one ship wrote a letter to a newspaper back home to warn others of the hardships. "Last year," he wrote, "one of the ships was driven about the ocean for twenty-four weeks, and of its one hundred and fifty passengers, more than one hundred starved to death. To satisfy their hunger, they caught mice and rats; and a mouse brought half a gulden."[13]

Reports are common of anywhere from a quarter to a half of the passengers falling ill and dying at sea, their corpses slipped overboard. There is even one account of a vessel that reached Philadelphia with only 50 of its 400 original passengers alive.[14] When the Brunners' ship reached Philadelphia on September 11, 1729 after ten weeks at sea, providentially every member of the family had survived although son Johannes was listed on the ship's manifest as "sick."[15]

Once ships reached port, passengers who had paid their own way could disembark. The less wealthy who had agreed to become indentured servants, or redemptioners, were required to stay aboard and wait for some local person to "buy" them, as the practice was termed, from the captain. While redemptioners waited on the ship, a doctor would come aboard to see whether any might be carrying communicable diseases.

We do not know whether the Brunners were redemptioners or had paid the ship captain enough money to go free immediately. We do know that they would spend about seven years—the length of many indentures—in Pennsylvania without leaving any record of attempting to purchase land.

Four days after landing, Joseph and Christian Getzendanner, his son-in-law, were taken to the courthouse where they signed two papers.[16] One renounced allegiance to any foreign leader and the other affirmed loyalty to the British crown.[17] Only after the redemptioners had signed the papers and were marched back to the ship did prospective employers board and hope to find the sort of person or persons he might wish to buy. It could take days or weeks before every passenger was allowed to go ashore for good. If there were no takers for some passengers, ship captains placed advertisements in the newspaper. During the 1720s and 1730s, redemptioners were typically sold for four or five years of labor at £10 per head. (Again, it is not possible accurately to convert these figures to today's money.)[18]

A typical advertisement that a ship captain placed in a newspaper to sell passengers who could not pay for their passage.

The system of selling—and sometimes reselling—immigrants was so much abused that some religious groups, especially the Mennonites, branded it the "German Slave Trade." Their efforts to stamp it out had little success because the Palatine peoples were desperate to escape their homeland at any cost.[19]

We do not know what happened to the Brunners at this point in their journey. Were they free upon landing in America? If not, were they all taken by the same "owner" or was the family split up? Were their masters kind or cruel? Did they work on rural farms or in city shops? Did they learn new trades, perhaps skills that would serve them in the future? One common obligation many masters had in their part of the bargain was to give the released redemptioner a set of tools of the trade they had been practicing and a suit of clothes. In any event, the Brunners would not reach Maryland for another seven years.

4

Pennsylvania

Philadelphia, besides being the largest city in America, was second in the English-speaking world only to London. It was the main port with ocean-going ships sailing up Delaware Bay into the Delaware River and to the city. The most reliable estimates put its population at around 11,000 when the Brunners landed.[1] It was the time of Benjamin Franklin, who was publishing his *Pennsylvania Gazette.* In 1732 Franklin even started a German language newspaper, one of five in the city serving the burgeoning German population, but it failed after two months.[2]

So numerous were Palatine people in the city, in fact, that many signs in the streets were bilingual. That aroused fears among the English. No less enlightened a figure than Franklin himself wrote to his American colleagues that if the tide of Germans was not diverted to other provinces, "all the advantages we have, will, in my opinion, be not able to preserve our language, and even our government will become precarious." He need not have feared; a generation later German Americans, except for pacifist sects, would be among the most ardent to rebel against British rule. They knew a little something about oppressive rulers.

Franklin's early antipathy toward Germans found frequent expression in his writings. He once wrote that they were "of the most Ignorant Stupid Sort."[3] On the other hand, Franklin's friend, Benjamin Rush, a Philadelphia physician and also one of the Founding Fathers, had a better opinion. He characterized the German settlers as among "the best members of Republican governments" and praised their "Republican virtues of industry and economy." He called them "skillful cultivators of the earth."[4]

The countryside beyond Philadelphia would have proved a welcoming new home for the Brunners. The rich soils and climate were similar to those in the Palatinate and supported the same kinds of crops. By the time the family arrived, a generation of Palatine peoples had already settled in the farmlands outside Philadelphia and especially to the west in Lancaster County. By 1733 a road connected Philadelphia to the new town of Lancaster.[5] The new settlement would become a center of various tradesmen such as blacksmiths, tanners, and woodwrights (who made wagons and furniture). No record of the Brunners' time in Pennsylvania has come to light, but if they were indentured, as seems likely, the family members probably worked on farms and in shops in the Philadelphia/Lancaster region.

As Rush noted, the Germans had gained a reputation as excellent farmers. Their well-built barns, tidy farmyards, healthy livestock and high crop yields eventually won broad admiration. "It is pretty to behold our back Settlements," a Welsh-born surveyor wrote in 1753, "where the barns are as large as pallaces, while the owners live in log hutts; a sign, tho, of thriving farmers." [6] That characterization spawned a stereotype of German farmsteads that was seldom accurate. German homes and barns could vary greatly in relative size and degree of polish.

Despite such variations, it is clear that Germans were introducing a new European culture to America, the first in the colonies to differentiate itself from the English way of life that had taken root along the Atlantic seaboard.[7] Multiculturalism among white settlers was born, even if it would not take that name for centuries.

If not indentured on a German farm, the Brunners may well have been working for pay to accumulate funds to buy their own land in the area. Either way, the family does appear to have improved its station after a few years. Official land records in Philadelphia and Lancaster County show, for example, that the Getzendanners (Christian and Anna Barbara Brunner), had a parcel surveyed about five years after reaching Philadelphia.[8] The delay suggests that they were indeed redemptioners. No record has turned up, however, to indicate that any of the other Brunners had acquired land of their own.[9]

Toward the end of the family's years in Pennsylvania, records show that their lives were progressing ahead socially if not economically. On April 13, 1736, Joseph and Cathrina's younger daughter Maria Cathrina, now about 19, married Stephen Remsberger, 24, who had come from Germany a few years before the Brunners. In keeping with the German custom of the time, she took her husband's last name and added a suffix indicating the feminine form—Remsbergerin.

The wedding gives us the last known evidence for Cathrina in America. She seems to be listed among the witnesses to the ceremony, though there appears to be an error in how her name was written. Interestingly the wedding was not officiated by a clergyman but by a justice of the peace.[10] That was the practice among Quakers of that time who had no formal clergy. It's not likely that either party had become Quaker, but more probably that a Reformed clergyman was not available. This was shortly before the rest of the Brunner clan was to move away.

Just a month after the wedding the Brunners—except for the newlyweds—left Pennsylvania and headed to Maryland. Perhaps they had worked off their indentures. Perhaps they were unable to save enough money to buy their own land. That would not be surprising because so many immigrants were flooding into William Penn's commonwealth—and so many from prior years had regained their freedom and were putting down roots—that they were bidding up the price of land year by year.[11]

Competition for acreage in Lancaster County was further increased because colonial rulers blocked westward expansion. They forbade pioneers from pushing the frontier beyond the Susquehanna River, the county's western boundary. By treaty that land still belonged to the Indians.[12] Prospects must have looked better to the southwest.

5
Opportunity in Maryland

Like Pennsylvania, Maryland was a proprietary colony. In this case the proprietor was Charles Calvert, the fifth Lord Baltimore. In 1727, he "patented," or granted, some 7,000 acres of wilderness west of the Monocacy River in today's Frederick County to Benjamin Tasker. He was a prominent English businessman in Annapolis who had also served as the town's mayor, and he was a land speculator.[1]

He named his possession Tasker's Chance and hoped to rent parcels to settlers. In those days Maryland land owners still followed the ancient British feudal system in which the landlord was literally lord of the land. As such he retained claim on the property, supposedly in perpetuity, but for all practical purposes the occupant had possession, although he was required to pay an annual or semi-annual rent or, as it was called, quit-rent. Though the cost was modest, few English people were taking up residence in Tasker's Chance.[2]

Five years later Lord Baltimore, no doubt aware of the abundance German settlers were bringing to Pennsylvania, sweetened the offer for the entire province to attract more tenants and, of course, to increase his income. He ruled that any settler could have 200 acres of land and live on it free of charge for three years before having to pay anything. In addition, each person between the ages of 15 and 30 could have an additional 100 acres at no cost for three years. After that the settler would have to pay four shillings sterling for every 100 acres each year thereafter.[3] In four years' time most of the extended Brunner family, surely aware of Baltimore's offer, would make the trek from Pennsylvania.

In 1732, the Maryland Assembly was farsighted enough to introduce the concept of paper money, becoming the first colony to make it a permanent element of the economy. Some paper money was used to pay for government projects such as roads, and some was simply given away to each family, making it simpler for them to buy and sell things without needing to hand over a quantity of tobacco, which until then was the chief means of exchange. The paper money stimulated the economy to grow rapidly.[4] That and the offer of "free" land may eventually have made Maryland attractive to the Brunners.

Charles Calvert, aka the 5th Lord Baltimore.
Courtesy Enoch Pratt Free Library, Baltimore.

No first-person description of the new land is known, but the popular notion that the wilderness of that time was uninterrupted forest is wrong. The region was a mix of hardwood and coniferous forests with large clearings, often left behind by the Native American practice of burning large areas to encourage game and to make sunny places for crops. So large were some fires that there is a report from much earlier times of a ship captain smelling smoke 40 miles offshore. The treeless burned-over areas, mostly turned to prairie, were known as barrens, a term that led some people to think that the soil was poor. That belief also discouraged the English from moving inland.[5]

Tasker's Chance was a land of gently rolling hills bordered by the Monocacy, a fairly substantial river, and crossed by smaller streams, including Carroll Creek. Not far to the west stood the Catoctin Mountains, a part of the Blue Ridge range of the ancient and worn-down Appalachian Mountains. Archaeological finds indicate that native peoples had lived in the region at various times over several thousand years, at least in small camps. A dig on Carroll Creek near the site of today's Schifferstadt house turned up the remains of an ancient hearth with animal bones and flakes of stone from tool making.[6] No evidence has turned up that Native Americans were settled in the area when the Brunners arrived.

An abundance of large game such as elk, deer and bison roamed the forests and meadows. Smaller game such as turkeys and rabbits were also available. Bears, wolves and even cougars prowled the area.[7] Eventually, as was the case with Indians across the Americas, smallpox, influenza and other diseases accidentally introduced by European explorers and settlers caused devastating epidemics, wiping out huge numbers of native peoples.[8] Large swaths of America became uninhabited or only lightly populated.

To the Brunners and other Germans who could not afford the increasingly costly land in Pennsylvania, Lord Baltimore's offer must have been attractive. And, despite the "barrens" label, the soil was good in central Maryland. A settler could be a homesteader—find a nice piece of land, put down roots and get established before having to come up with a penny.

The prospects lured many Germans to head west from Lancaster County and then south along the Monocacy River Valley, following an old Indian path that had been widened to accommodate wagons drawn by horses and oxen. It came to be called the German Monocacy Road. Actually, several different routes were given that name. Moreover, "Monocacy" came to be the label applied to the entire area. Some older writers suggest that Monocacy named a specific settlement or town, sometimes said to be lost

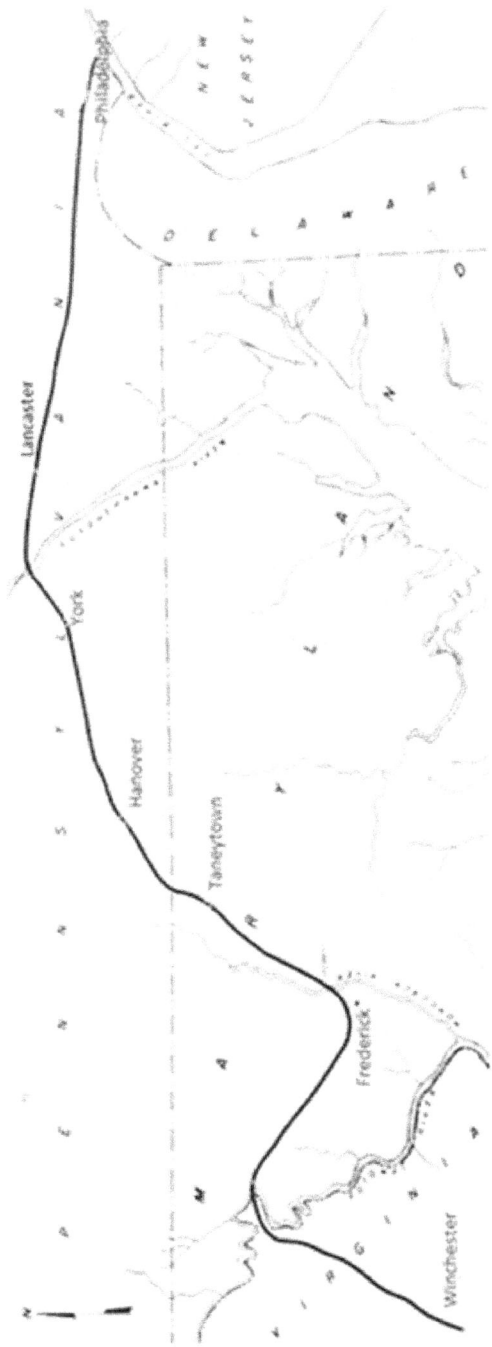

The German / Monocacy Road from Philadelphia, through Lancaster, then along the Monocacy River valley. Near Frederick Town it turns to the northwest and then southwest near present day Williamsport.

and sometimes thought to be near present-day Creagerstown. Others say now that the word always denoted the region through which the river passed.[9]

Before reaching the area of present-day Frederick some Germans turned west to pioneer Hagerstown while others went south across the Potomac River into Virginia's Shenandoah Valley. But many, including the Brunners and their relatives the Sturms and the Getzendanners evidently liked the look of what is now central Frederick County. They might have thought that Monocacy resembled their homeland in the Rhine Valley. In fact, there are similarities in topography, climate, vegetation and soil types.

The Brunners arrived in 1736, probably in May, just weeks after the marriage of Maria Cathrina and Stephen Remsberger. They selected farm sites between the Catoctin Mountains to the west and the site, already laid out, of what would become Frederick Town a mile to the east.[10] Their choices happened to be in Tasker's Chance, although it would be nearly a decade before they took deeds to the land on which they had settled and established farms. The Brunners were among the earliest settlers in the wilderness that is now Frederick County.

6

A New Brunner Home

If Joseph and Cathrina followed the usual pattern that guided pioneering homesteaders, their first task was to select a suitable home site. It should have easy access to water and to reasonably level ground on which to plant crops. And it should not be far from tall and straight trees that could be felled to build a log house. Like most German settlers, the Brunners knew that the richest soils lay beneath dense, old forests, so it seems likely that they chose land within or next to an established forest. Felled trees supplied both building materials and firewood.

Unlike the pattern in the old country where nearly all homes were clustered in villages and farmers trekked to their fields in outlying areas, most homesteaders in America chose to build on widely separated parcels of land. No doubt that practice accorded with the sense of independence and self-reliance the Germans brought with them.[1] Still, the Brunners may have known that a town was forming just a mile away.

Everywhere in the young America outside of cities, log cabins were the first and easiest kind of home to erect. Two or three men can build a one-room cabin in a few days. The floor was commonly earthen and the pitched roof was made of overlapping planks split out of oak logs. A key goal was to have a cabin closed in before the first winter.[2] Until then pioneers usually slept in or under their wagons.

Joseph and Cathrina picked a spot and named their plantation for their home town in the old country. In official records, it is spelled Sheverstadt.[3] The three grown sons settled short distances away. To the south Henderick, or Henry as he came to be called, named his place Carrolls Creek for the watercourse that ran through all the Brunner farms.[4] John (to give him the Anglicized version of Johannes) took land just north of his father and dubbed it What-You-Will.[5] North of John was Jacob's farm which he, possibly more pleased with his choice, called Rich Levells.[6] Daughter Anna Barbara and her husband, Christian Getzendanner, settled a little farther away.[7]

Two or three years later, the last two members of the family moved from Pennsylvania to Maryland. Daughter Maria Cathrina and her husband Stephen Remsberger settled on a parcel a little farther from the others and called it, for reasons not clear, Mortallity.[8] Somewhat later Stephen bought another piece of land that he called Dear Bought.[9] That name survives today as a suburban housing development on the same land just north of the city of Frederick. All the farms were in the large parcel of near-wilderness called Tasker's Chance.

Joseph Brunner's log house probably sat within the footprint of today's Schifferstadt Architectural Museum, directly below the brick addition that stands today, built in about 1867. That building contains the museum shop and on the top floor the office of the Frederick County Landmarks Foundation. The ground floor, with its very old and possibly original brick floor, contains an open-hearth fireplace, which may have served Joseph's log cabin. An insurance policy written in 1848 refers to a log house on the site.[10]

Joseph chose well. In those days Carroll Creek ran near the base of a small slope that dips away from today's museum. (The creek was rerouted farther away in modern times.)[11] The spot may already have been in a clearing. If not, he would have felled trees to create a clearing, trimming up the logs to make his house.

We know from recent archaeological research that Native Americans visited the banks of the creek and stayed long enough to leave a few stone tool remnants. That suggests it was an attractive place for a hunting party to camp for a few days or perhaps for a family to live for a season. The creek would have been a good place to fish, both for the natives and the settlers. The Indians used weirs to trap fish, and the Germans may have copied that method.[12]

At 58 Joseph could have been fit enough to do much of the

construction himself, but he had the help of his youngest son, Elias, who was then about 13 years old. Quite likely the older Brunner boys helped Joseph and each other to build their first homes. While log cabins may strike people today as primitive, they can be made quite comfortable. Spaces between logs were chinked with a mixture of clay and moss. In time the exterior often was covered with shingles split out of oak log sections or longer vertical boards. Inside walls were often plastered and whitewashed to make the interior brighter. Floors of such homes often were earthen but in time covered with wooden planks split out of logs or even bricks.[13] Fireplaces served for cooking and heating.

For the next 17 years Joseph likely continued to live in his log house, son Elias growing into manhood. Joseph's wife, Cathrina, surely was with them in the early years, but no record of her in Maryland has turned up. As mentioned earlier, she was alive in Pennsylvania a month before the family headed south. It appears that she died some time before 1753, when Joseph sold Schifferstadt to Elias (more about that in later chapters). Records of real estate sales in those days normally name wives, who were required to agree to forego their right to inherit the property. Cathrina's name does not appear in the bill of sale as giving up her "dower right."[14]

If Joseph and Elias lived in their house as just the two of them, life could have been difficult. The division of labor between the sexes on a farm was fairly rigid in those days. Men's work focused on the fields and the livestock while woman's work centered on young children, house and hearth. There were some tasks in which men and women worked together, such as the time-critical harvesting of wheat and other grains.[15] In the absence of a housewife, Joseph may well have had a "hired girl" to take that role.

Another source of labor on some farms was enslaved people. We know of no evidence that Joseph had slaves, but it is clear that at least two of his sons did. According to Henry's will of December 24, 1775, he owned one slave, named Samuel, whom he bequeathed to his son, then to be freed after 15 more years of servitude.[16] John's will lists four slaves—named Fortune, Will, Nat and Sal. All four were to go to John's son. There is no mention of manumission.[17]

Doubtless Joseph and Elias built a barn and acquired livestock. Typical farms of those days had a cow or two for milk, cheese and butter; pigs

27

for meat; chickens, ducks or geese for eggs, meat and feathers to stuff the mattresses that the Germans favored, which they called featherbeds. They may have had an ox for plowing and dragging felled trees for construction and firewood as well as one or more horses and a wagon for travel to neighboring farmsteads such as those of the sons and daughters and to mills that would grind their grain into flour.[18]

And with Frederick Town growing just a mile away, the Brunners surely visited now and then to sell surplus produce and to buy craft-made iron tools, nails, hinges, pots and commodities such as salt, sugar and gunpowder. The town was predominantly German, so the Brunner men likely visited inns to catch up on the latest news.

Quite probably Joseph and Elias hunted wild game for meat and hides. Along with deer and elk there were turkeys, some said to weigh as much as 30 pounds. And there were low-flying clouds of now-extinct passenger pigeons, which some settlers said could be knocked out of the air with a stick.[19]

The open land was used as pasture for the livestock and plowed for the usual crops, ones they knew from the Rhineland and from Pennsylvania—oats, wheat, rye, barley, flax and hemp as well as familiar vegetables such as cabbage, potatoes and turnips. A vegetable and herb garden probably was laid out near the house, in the traditional four-square design (a large square enclosing four smaller squares) with raised beds and a picket fence to keep out rabbits and woodchucks.[20] No doubt they planted apple trees for eating, for cider (the fermented kind, which stores well) and for slicing to make apple butter and for drying to make schnitz, a favorite ingredient that sweetens many traditional German recipes. In some rental contracts landlords required each farm to put in 100 apple trees. Such requirements went along with terms specifying the dimensions of houses and barns that must be built.[21]

As the farms of the Brunners and other early settlers were developing quietly, their land was the subject of ambitious business negotiations in Annapolis, the faraway economic and legal center of the colony.

In 1744 Daniel Dulany, an Annapolis-based lawyer, politician and land speculator, visited Tasker's Chance and saw it as a land of opportunity, especially for himself. Dulany was an Irish immigrant who arrived in Maryland in 1703 as a redemptioner and was indentured to an Annapolis lawyer, eventually learning to be one himself. In fact, Dulany rose from poverty to become one of the richest men in Maryland, both through his law practice and land speculation.[22]

In a letter to Lord Baltimore, Dulany called Tasker's Chance "a most delightful Country, a Country My Lord, that Equals (if it does not exceed) any in America for natural advantages, such as rich and fertile soil, well furnished with timber of all sorts, abounding with limestone, and stone fit for building, good slate and some Marble, and to Crown all, very healthy."[23]

Dulany envisioned great promise for the area and in 1744 bought Tasker's Chance from Benjamin Tasker for £2,000.[24] More than a speculator like Tasker, Dulany became a developer, carving his new possession into 26 farm-sized parcels to rent and, eventually, to sell. Dulany also selected one parcel to become a town. To settle his countryside and populate the town that he envisioned, Dulany specifically wanted Germans. He called them "the fittest people that can be to Settle a New Country."[25] No doubt he had already visited their homes and fields, perhaps even the four adjoining farms of the Brunners, which had been established and operating for about eight years.

The Irishman recognized that the Maryland interior was not as well suited to growing tobacco as were the tidewater lands around his base in Annapolis, though some farmers did grow a little tobacco as a cash crop. Dulany believed that other crops would do better, especially the cereal grains and pasturage that were typical of the Palatinate and of Pennsylvania, where German settlers were thriving. Besides the Brunner farms, there already were a few other German farms when Dulany arrived, and he may have seen what crops they already were growing.

Quite possibly, Dulany's surveyor drew property lines between neighboring Brunner farms. In 1746, Joseph Brunner officially bought the 303 acres of Schifferstadt, paying £10 in the Maryland currency of the time. In that same year at least 16 other farms were delineated by Dulany's surveyor.[26] The purchase money went to Dulany, and the annual quit-rents went to Lord Baltimore even though he had relinquished ownership of the 7,000 acres of land contained in the Tasker's Chance parcel in 1727, when he granted a patent for this land to Benjamin Tasker.[27] Maryland was one of only a few American colonies that kept a version of the ancient

English feudal system in which the quit-rent, a tax calculated on the area of land occupied by a resident, continued to be paid until the American Revolution.[28]

Beyond farms, Dulany believed his new possession would need a commercial hub and so took one of the parcels situated on Carroll's Creek, as it was then named, for a town. He divided it into 351 city lots, each measuring 60 feet by 393 feet.[29] Many were sold to Germans, but for several decades Dulany kept all the positions of Frederick Town's political power in the hands of his Irish family. Germans were the most numerous ethnic group, followed by Scots-Irish (people from the mainly Protestant region of northern Ireland). Possibly there already were a few homes and shops, but the influx of German settlers in the surrounding area told Dulany that the village could become a thriving town.

Among the earlier settlers to buy in the new town was Johannes (or John) Thomas Schley, who emigrated from Germany in 1745 and landed in Annapolis.[30] He soon headed west to Frederick Town and began paying quit-rent on four of Dulany's town lots in that same year. Though sometimes called the founder of what was to become Frederick City, others had already settled in the town—enough that local residents three years earlier had petitioned the Maryland Assembly to make Frederick Town the county seat of a new Frederick County.

Early on, however, Schley did become one of the town's leading citizens, serving as a schoolmaster and a longtime innkeeper, holding the required license to operate an "ordinary," as some taverns and inns were known in colonial America.[31] And he was a founding member of the Reformed Church to which the Brunners belonged. He was a lay preacher and must have been impressive in the pulpit because a traveling Reformed minister who visited Frederick Town, Michael Schlatter, wrote of Schley, "They have the best schoolmaster that I have met in America. He spares neither labor nor pains in instructing the young and edifying the congregation, according to his ability, by means of singing and reading the word of God and printed sermons on every Lord's Day."[32] Printed sermons attest that a fair number of the German settlers were literate. Schley went on to become the church organist, a composer, a calligrapher in the German style called fraktur, a founder of the town's first fire company, and a lieutenant in the Frederick militia.[33]

Daniel Dulany bought the 7,000 acres of Tasker's Chance and divided
it into these 26 parcels. He chose the southernmost in which to lay out
the first streets of Frederick Town. The male Brunners occupied four
adjacent farms. One daughter married Stephen Ramsburg.
*Adapted from Pioneers of Old Monocacy, by Grace L. Tracey and John
P. Dern. Courtesy of the Historical Society of Carroll County,
Westminster, Maryland.*

Daniel Dulany's foresight proved extraordinary. Within five years of his selling the first lots, Frederick Town would have a population estimated at 1,000, making it the largest municipality in Maryland, topping Annapolis, the second largest, by 200 people. (Baltimore, which got a later start, was still a small village with about 150 residents at this time.)[34]

By 1755, ten years after Dulany laid out the town, an English visitor wrote that it had 200 houses and two churches, one English and one German. He noted that the inhabitants were "chiefly Dutch," using a label based on a common misunderstanding of the word Deutsch.[35] That same year an Englishwoman visiting the town wrote in her diary that it was "a very Pleasant place most of the people are Duch." [36]

Frederick Town and the surrounding countryside were, in fact, predominantly German and would stay that way for generations. German-language newspapers would circulate in the county well into the 1800s.

In 1753, Joseph Brunner was 75 years old and no doubt had been turning over more of the farm work to Elias, now aged 30. This youngest Brunner son had married a woman named Albertina (or in some records, Alberdina) five years earlier.[37] Given Joseph's age, it is likely that Elias and Albertina lived at Schifferstadt, helping to look after the old man, who by this time seems to have been a widower.

According to a deed dated January 17, 1753, Joseph sold the farm to Elias for £200 in "current money" of the day.[38] In other words, Elias handed over that much Maryland currency to his father. It may seem curious that the old man didn't simply give the farm to his son or will it to him. One possibility is that Joseph needed money and, evidently, Elias had it. Or Joseph may have wanted to share the proceeds with his other sons. One indication that Cathrina had died by this time is that she is not mentioned in the deed that Elias took. As was noted earlier, she would have had a "dower right" to inherit the property and her husband could not sell the place without her consenting to give up that right.

It appears that Joseph died sometime between 1753 and 1756. In that latter year the German Reformed church in Frederick Town enacted a new ordinance that was signed by church elders, including the Brunner sons but not their father, who also had been an elder.[39] The absence of his name from that document suggests that Joseph may have been too ill or infirm to sign. Or he may have died by then. No direct evidence of Joseph's death has come to light.

Today's stone house would not be built for another five years, so Elias and Albertina probably continued to live in the old log house or perhaps a newer, bigger one built years earlier when the old one no longer met their needs. By then the young couple had two small sons, Stephan and Peter.[40] In 1758, it appears, Elias built the house that stands today.

7

Brunners on the Record, Part 1

Between the arrival of the Brunner clan in Maryland in the spring of 1736 and the 1750s, when hostilities between British and French troops began brewing on the western frontier, family members show up several times in official records. Clearly they had begun taking part in the civic and religious life of their adopted homeland. But the earliest known record confirms that the family's first encounter with officialdom was not entirely happy.

In those days there was a law requiring inhabitants each year to give a local justice of the peace at least three squirrels' scalps or crows' heads for each taxable person, which meant each adult. The Prince George's County Court Record (today's Frederick County was part of Prince George's) for 1736 shows Brunners as being "deficient in bringing in their Quotas of Crows and Squirrels heads according to act of assembly." Three Brunners are on this list: Joseph along with his two eldest sons, Jacob and John. Other family members would run afoul of the same law in ensuing years. Joseph's and Cathrina's son-in-law, Stephen Ramsburg, showed up on the list in 1740; Henry, the third Brunner son, was listed in 1741. For each deficiency the violator was fined two pounds of tobacco.[1]

Why the law? There were so many squirrels and crows about that they were causing significant damage to planters' crops—pulling up corn and wheat seedlings and eating ears of corn on the stalks. Colonial officials thought the problem could be relieved by requiring each person to kill a few varmints. Wolves were also a problem, but the law did not require people to produce an entire dead wolf. Instead of the stick, the law offered a carrot—200 pounds of tobacco as a bounty for each wolf's head brought in.[2]

Alas, there was another instance when a Brunner ran afoul of the law. In 1739 John Brunner, the second son of Joseph and Cathrina, was hauled before a local magistrate for "Breach of Sabbath." It seems that a man named George Howes turned him in.

In those days Maryland had an established religion. Lord Baltimore had decreed that the colony was officially Roman Catholic, but Protestants later took control of Maryland's colonial government and switched the official religion to the Church of England, or Anglicanism. In the hinterlands of Frederick Town, however, other sects were tolerated as long as they observed basic Christian practices such as keeping the Sabbath.

The record does not describe John's offense in detail, but he went to trial in 1740. According to the court record, "the premises being seen by the Court, it is considered said John Brunner be fined, forfeit and pay 200 pounds of tobacco to the County for its use. Brunner paid the Clerk twenty shillings in Bills of Credit in discharge of the fine and is dismist paying fees."[3]

In that same year, the Brunners took a more consequential step. On May 3, 1740 all the Brunners officially swore allegiance to Lord Baltimore, thus becoming naturalized and gaining the right to own property, a right they would exercise in 1746, all of them taking deeds to their farms from Daniel Dulany, the owner and developer of this region of the county.[4]

In 1741, the Prince George's County Court appointed the new citizen Henry Brunner "overseer" of a road from the "top of Catoctin Mountain to the Monocacy Waggon Road ford near Thomas Beatty's," a stretch of several miles.[5] Such a duty was part of a general system, before the existence of public works departments, giving, in this instance, Henry, the responsibility to see that the unpaved path for wagons and horses was kept clear of encroaching vegetation, fallen trees and washouts.

In 1763, Jacob, Henry's older brother, was appointed "roads commissioner," which may have given him broader authority over the thoroughfares that were becoming ever more important to the growing number of townspeople, outlying farms and through traffic from surrounding areas headed for Annapolis and other towns to the east.[6]

In these same years many settlers began to chafe at being part of a vast Prince George's County that stretched from the present area of Prince George's County east of Washington, D.C., to the western tip of Maryland—including today's Montgomery, Frederick, Washington, Allegany and Garrett Counties. To transact some kinds of business, residents had to travel more than 50 miles to the county seat at Upper Marlborough (now spelled Upper Marlboro), a round trip that would take most of a week out of a farmer's busy work schedule.

With Frederick Town continuing to grow larger than the provincial capital of Annapolis, several members of the Brunner family joined in a 1742 petition to the Assembly asking that Prince George's County be split, carving off a new "Frederick County" as a separate jurisdiction with Frederick Town as the county seat. Among the signers of that petition were Joseph Brunner and his sons Jacob, John and Elias, as well as Joseph's son-in-law Christian Getzendanner who, by this time, had moved to Maryland with his wife Anna Barbara, née Brunner.[7] The people who fled the Palatinate as desperate refugees were now exercising their rights as free citizens in their new homeland.

The colonial Assembly appointed a committee to study the matter and began a process that took six years, much of the time taken up by disagreements over where to draw the boundary. Finally, in 1748 the Assembly did grant the wish of the Brunners and their neighbors and create Frederick County as its own unit of government.[8] It left Prince George's with approximately the boundaries it has today. The newly created Frederick County comprised all the rest, stretching from today's Montgomery County, today a Washington, D.C. suburb, to the western end of the province, today's Garrett County.

Ever since they arrived in Maryland, the Brunners had been active in the German Reformed Church that had come to Frederick Town with the many Palatine immigrants. A majority of German immigrants were Lutherans. Of those who were not Lutheran, most belonged to the Reformed Faith.[9]

The year of 1748 would prove to be one of the most eventful in the religious lives of the Brunner clan for several reasons. For one, the Reformed congregation had grown large enough by that year to need a proper meeting house. Daniel Dulany, had given them a lot in town, just as he had to the

Lutherans and to the English church.[10] The Reformed lot was just west of Market Street and stretched from West Patrick Street to Church Street. A wooden meeting house was built at one end of the lot, facing Patrick. In 1764 it was replaced by a stone building at the other end of the lot, facing Church Street.[11]

Brunner family members were ardent defenders of their Reformed faith. In that same year of 1748, for example, four of the men, all elders of the local congregation, saw a serious problem confronting their church. Joseph, his son Jacob, and his two sons-in-law, Stephen Remensperger (as it was spelled in the record), and Christian Getzendanner wanted help. They sent a letter to an official of their church who was then in Philadelphia. The recipient was Michael Schlatter, a German Reformed clergyman who had been sent by church authorities in Europe to assist in developing his denomination's congregations in America.

As with many religious groups on the frontier, Reformed followers in Frederick Town were getting by without a full-time clergyman. Lay leaders would organize services, often for several months at a stretch, waiting for a cleric to come by and perform the services proper only to a man of the cloth.

The problem in 1748 was that a rival Christian sect was luring away Reformed members. According to the elders' letter, two members of the German Baptist Brethren, one of the German sects similar to the Mennonites and Amish, were persuading Reformed believers to convert to their more conservative faith. The practice of baptism was a key difference. The Reformed church, like Catholics and Lutherans, simply poured water over the foreheads of babies. By contrast, the Baptist Brethren, also called Dunkers, insisted that a person should be baptized by total immersion and not until he or she was old enough to decide whether to join the church, usually not until the teenage years. The Dunkers, like the Mennonites and Amish, were Anabaptists. As described in the 1660 book *The Martyr's Mirror,* Anabaptists gained that name, meaning re-baptiser, because they offered converts the chance to be baptised again when they were old enough to decide for themselves.

The Brunners reminded Rev. Schlatter that it had been ten months since he visited and held Holy Communion. Could he please come quickly and advise how to prevent further sectarian piracy.[12]

Schlatter responded, visiting Frederick on his way from Philadelphia to the Shenandoah Valley. He held services at the Reformed church on May 7 and again a week later. No account of his advice has turned up.[13]

There is a curiosity in the record. Although many sources attest that Jacob and the other Brunners belonged to the Reformed church, a written history of the rival Brethren church (yet another German sect) in Frederick County states that in 1750 Jacob Brunner became active as a preacher for two Dunker congregations. According to the church history, generally thought to be credible, the man who complained in 1748 about Dunkers luring away Reformed members may, just two years later, have become a Dunker himself. Had he been converted? Or had his views softened only to the point of helping out the Dunkers because, like many churches, they had no resident pastor? The teachings of the two groups were similar, except for the rules on baptism. Did Schlatter advise Jacob to be more tolerant? We may never know.[14]

Also in 1748, Stephen Ransberger, he of the highly variable last name, filed a deposition on behalf of "a Great Number of the Germans and some others" protesting the way the sheriff was treating them. Ransberger told the governor and his council that the sheriff was extorting money from them when he collected quit-rents, a service he performed for owners of properties distant from the capital, where the owners and landlords lived. He said the sheriff's actions reminded the Germans how they had been mistreated in their native land.

As the official record put it, "a Great Number of the Germans and some others were so much alarmed by the Sheriffs Proceedings, that Several of them have already Left the Province, and others have declared, that as soon as they could Sell what they were Possessed off, they would go away, many of the Germans declaring, that they being Oppressed in their Native Country, Induced them to Leave it, and that they were Apprehensive of being Equally oppressed here, and that therefore they would go away to avoid it."

The deposition lists many of the settlers by name along with the quit-rent they owed and the fee the sheriff was charging on top of that. Jacob Brunner's situation was typical. He owed a quit-rent of just 6 pence but the sheriff demanded an additional 15 shillings from him. In this case the sheriff was pocketing an amount 30 times as much as would go to the landlord.

The governor's response was simply to tell the sheriff to stop doing this. It doesn't seem that the governor's mild instruction was effective.[15] Two years later, in 1750, Jacob Brunner filed another complaint saying that he was charged more than he owed. The court rejected his petition.[16]

On October 20, 1748, came another official action that shows some members of the family could look beyond the demands of their farms. They wanted to travel back to the old country to visit relatives and friends. The governor of Maryland, Samuel Ogle, granted a kind of passport to Jacob Brunner, his brother-in-law Stephen Remsperger, and their friends Nicholas Benedick and Henry Thomas. It appears that they did make the trip because the German Reformed church in Frederick, today called the Evangelical Reformed Church-United Church of Christ, has a record book with this inscription, translated from the German: "Johann Jacob Brunner bought this writing book for 50 Kreuzer at Frankfurt-am-Main, 16 Apr. 1749." No entries were made in the book until the first pastor was installed in 1753.[17]

One day in the fall of 1750, Joseph Brunner chanced upon a stray horse. As it happens, that was not so unusual. There were so many stray horses in the region that Maryland had a law "to redress the great Evil accruing to this Province by the Multiplicity of useless Horses, Mares, and Colts, that run in the Woods." The law said that anybody who captured a stray could keep it if he took the animal to the next court session to be seen by the magistrate and have the animal's brand recorded.[18] That's what Joseph did, and Maryland's official records for October 25, 1750, still show that the animal bore this brand:

Information in the Frederick County Land Records offers a glimpse of another element of life in colonial Maryland. In the absence of such later institutions as banks, people formed *ad hoc* mutual aid groups. In 1751, for example, a man named Conradt Keller owed £112 to Daniel Dulany. A considerable sum that, for example, is more than half the price that would be paid two years later for the entire 303 acres of the Schifferstadt farm. Keller didn't have the money. So Joseph Brunner and seven other friends of Keller pooled their resources to lend him £112.

But to make the transaction proper, Keller had to put up collateral. He agreed to "sell" certain goods to the eight farmers: "a wagon, horses, steers, calves, heifers, hay and plow irons." The bill of sale says that four of the horses were branded with a C and one with HTS. The cattle's left ears were notched in the shape of a half-penny coin.[19] Two years later, according to another document, Keller paid back the money and the eight creditors yielded their claim on the collateral, which "were and still are in the possession of the said Conradt Keller." [20]

There were no banks, but there was a court that retained records making this transaction official. Not all the farmers who lent Keller money were German. The list of creditors includes some English names, suggesting that the famously insular Germans were, in fact, enjoying good relations with their non-German neighbors. Assimilation was happening.

The next time we see Brunners on the record is May of 1756. The four brothers signed a new church ordinance establishing responsibilities and benefits of church membership. That document proclaims that "no association of men can exist whole and be happy without due order." Without rules, it added, "Christian congregations in particular ... can not long exist in a manner pleasing to God." It was signed by all four: Jacob, John, Henry and Elias, as well as Stephen Ramsburg.[21]

Another sign that the Brunners were active in their church and community is that their names show up numerous times as sponsors and witnesses at various baptisms, confirmations and weddings in the German Reformed community.

The focus on faith did not exclude a serious interest in facts. Eight years earlier, for example, the Brunner family's German Reformed congregation had built a schoolhouse on the church lot.[22] In making serious efforts to encourage formal education, the Reformed congregation was well ahead of the rest of Frederick Town.[23] But for centuries in Europe, education had been interwoven with religion.[24] Children were taught to read so they could read the Bible, which was the principal book used in school. Church schools also taught arithmetic, often called ciphers.

Maryland as a whole would not make an official effort to create public schools until 1763. In August of that year, the colony's governor, Horatio Sharpe, wrote to Lord Baltimore, "it is really to be lamented that while such great things are done for the Support of Colleges & Academics in the neighbouring Colonies, there is not in this even one good [public as opposed to church-linked] Grammar School.[25]

The response was swift. Four months later the Maryland Assembly passed "An ACT for erecting a Public School in Frederick County." [26]

Swift, but in the rising tension preceding the American Revolution, not effective. "The Revolutionary War," historian Thomas J.C. Williams wrote in 1910, "put an effective stop to much effort in this direction [of establishing a public school] and it was not until 1797, well after the war, that a grant was made by the Maryland Assembly and the school was opened." The new institution was named the Frederick County School and College.[27]

8

War Terrorizes a Peaceful Valley

By the early 1750s, it appears that the extended Brunner family was well established in Frederick County, their farms thriving in the land of peace and freedom they had sought not so long ago. On the horizon, however, the drums of war were getting louder. Frederick Town and surrounding farms were near the edge of the frontier, and to the west were signs of growing danger. Fear and uncertainty began to grip settlers, especially those in scattered farms in the hinterlands of western Maryland.

Events would soon bring a young George Washington to Frederick Town, where he would meet with Benjamin Franklin and the British general Edward Braddock. In 1757, at least eight members of the Brunner family would be pulled into the struggle to defend their new homeland. It was a fight that would grow into an international conflict known as the Seven Years' War. The French and Indian War, as it became known in the U.S., was the American theater of that world war. It is a fascinating saga poorly known among modern day Americans.

The way the conflict unfolded in Frederick County would help shape attitudes toward British rule that eventually found expression in the Revolutionary War. The following historical context of that tumultuous time illuminates the Brunners' military service. No doubt these matters were topics of conversation at Frederick Town's taverns and around dinner tables as well.

In 1749, Great Britain and France made rival claims on land in the Ohio River Valley. Investors from British Virginia had formed the Ohio Company, hoping to make money selling supposedly vacant lands west of the Allegheny Mountains. The company would also set up Indian trading posts in those areas. But the French saw the same land as a route for commerce between their territories in Quebec and southern Louisiana.[1]

Complicating the situation was the fact that American Indians also occupied this territory and had come to depend on the traders' wares such as cooking pots and guns.[2] The French and the Indian tribes in their territory had a long history of coexistence, especially in Canada.[3] But when the British began pushing westward, displacing Indians and often dealing dishonestly with them, resentment grew. Many Indian tribes sided with the French. But as the war developed, several groups would fight with the British.

When the governor of Canada began building a string of forts to protect their north-south route, the Ohio Company's trading posts were seen as obstacles. French troops attacked these British posts, seized and imprisoned the traders.[4] In 1753, word came that the French were establishing fortifications at what was called the "forks of the Ohio" River, at present-day Pittsburgh. Robert Dinwiddie, Virginia's lieutenant governor and effectively the colony's ruling official, sent 21-year-old George Washington to persuade the French to vacate.[5]

An Indian scout leads a young George Washington to meet the French.

But Washington found the French soldiers well entrenched, having built several forts armed with cannon. The area was also populated by French settlers and Indians. It was reported that he was "received in a polite genteel Manner by the Commandant [General Legardeur St. Pierre] of the Fort" who told the young Virginian that he had been instructed "to keep possession, and to advance farther and fight those that opposed them." The commander also told Washington that "he had expected an Army to be sent for twelve Months past by the English, and that they were prepared for them; for he supposed they must knock it out, and he did not care how soon."[6]

Washington took the discouraging news back to Williamsburg, then the capital of Virginia. Dinwiddie, now expecting conflict, wrote to Governor Horatio Sharpe of Maryland to raise the alarm and to ask for financial help. The Maryland Assembly, though, failed to see a threat to its own territory and refused to authorize money to support Virginia.[7] As hostilities grew over coming years, Maryland would appropriate only minimal funding to secure the frontier and to protect settlers like the Brunners and the now-thriving village of Frederick Town.[8]

A year later, Washington was sent west again, this time to clear a path to the forks in order to rescue English traders who had been attacked.[9] At Great Meadows, an area some 50 miles from the French Fort Duquesne, Washington's men, including a small number of Mingo Indian fighters, ambushed a French force. The Virginians killed several of the French, including their commander, one Joseph Coulon de Villiers de Jumonville. As the first armed clash between British and French forces, and in the absence of any declaration of war on either side, this attack became an international incident.

Washington and his men fell back, regrouped, built a small stockade, which he called "Fort of Necessity." There the Virginians waited for reinforcements. Those never arrived. In time, the French attacked in large numbers, and Washington was forced to surrender and retreat to Virginia.[10]

The following year, the British government sent General Braddock from England with two regiments of regular troops. The Crown hoped that Braddock would quickly subdue the French and take back the disputed land. The general marched with one brigade to Frederick Town, and camped at the north end.[11] In town, he met with Franklin and Washington to plan the westward campaign.[12] It was Franklin's task to find horses and wagons for the expedition. In those days an army seldom traveled with all the equipment it would need. Instead it hoped to persuade civilians to lend or rent their own horses and wagons. In Frederick Town, Franklin later wrote, Braddock sat "impatiently waiting for the return of those he had sent thro' the back parts of Maryland and Virginia to collect waggons."[13]

Braddock was angry that not enough wagons could be procured. The number brought in, according to Franklin, "amounted only to twenty-five, and not all of those were in serviceable condition. The general and all the officers were surpris'd, declar'd the expedition was then at an end, being impossible; and exclaim'd against the [British] ministers for ignorantly landing them in a country destitute of the means of conveying their stores, baggage, etc., not less than one hundred and fifty waggons being necessary."[14]

To raise more wagons, Franklin placed advertisements in the newspapers of Lancaster, York and Cumberland Counties of Pennsylvania. "In two weeks," he wrote, "one hundred and fifty waggons with two hundred and fifty-nine carrying horses were on their march for the camp" in Frederick Town.[15]

One reason for the settlers' reluctance to cooperate was clear to Franklin's son, William. The young man wrote to his father of one bleak situation he witnessed in the spring of 1755 while at the mouth of Conococheague Creek in western Maryland where it empties into the Potomac River. He wrote that the army's confiscation of horses and wagons was a serious blow to farmers.

"Tis scarcely to be believed," William wrote, "what havock and oppression has been committed by the army in their march. Hardly a farmer in Frederic County has either Horse, Waggon or Servant to do the business of his plantation. Many are intirely ruined, not being able to plant their Corn, [a British term for grain in general] or do anything for their subsistence."

Nor were the horses treated well. William went on to say that the troops had kept the horses tied up for seven or eight days without allowing them to graze or bringing them fodder. "Many have died with hunger," Franklin went on, "after gnawing the tongues of the Waggon, to which they were fastened."[16]

Horses and wagons from the Brunner farms, 25 miles to the southeast, may well have been appropriated for the war effort, but we have no record of this.

Finally, Braddock and Washington met the enemy at the Battle of Monongahela near today's Pittsburgh and, despite all the wagons and horses, were soundly defeated by the French. Braddock was mortally wounded and died on the retreat.[17] His defeat left Maryland's western frontier defenseless until 1756-1757 when Governor Sharpe authorized building Fort Frederick with thick stone walls 41 miles west of Frederick Town. That and Fort Cumberland, an old stockade supply fort 90 miles west, were the only strongholds on the expansive Western Maryland frontier.[18]

The danger to those living on the frontier was real, and Braddock's failure to defeat the French unleashed a wave of Indian attacks on settlers in this sparsely inhabited region. Using tactics familiar today as guerrilla warfare and terrorism, Indians burned homes and murdered whole families.

An issue of the *Maryland Gazette*, dated April 1, 1756, contains a distressing narrative by a resident of Conococheague, a settlement on the Maryland/Pennsylvania border, near present day Hagerstown. As the story was told, Indians who had been hiding at the base of a tree, grabbed the bridle of a passing settler's horse, and commanded the man to dismount.

"Oh, what tongue can utter the Horror and Confusion which in an Instant overwhelmed me," the resident wrote. The man is forced to watch helplessly as a neighbor is scalped, then is taken to his own home where he and his wife are "commanded to depart. Here our Grief again renewed on leaving our House, Stock, Grain, and in short our All, behind us." The Indians then "set Fire to it … that in a few minutes, the whole was in a Blaze."[19] This is just one of many published reports of attacks on settlers in Western Maryland. Such tactics were meant to terrorize, and they did.

Washington mentions the effect in a letter to Lord Thomas Fairfax dated August 26, 1756. "The whole Settlement of Conogochieg in maryland, is fled; and there now remain only two families from thence to Fredericktown. That the maryland Settlements are all abandoned, is certainly fact, three hundred and fifty waggons had passed that place [Monocacy], to avoid the enemy, within the space of three days."[20]

An artist's conception of Indians capturing white children. In this case, the scene is based on an account of an incident in the Susquehanna Valley of Pennsylvania.

Although Washington calls the site of the huge wagon train Monocacy, it is not clear what place he was referring to. It is possible that it was a settlement called Monocacy, but if so, its location remains a mystery to historians. Many of those frightened, fleeing settlers likely passed through Frederick Town, some surely seeking refuge with residents of the town. The townspeople and, no doubt, the Brunner clan, experienced great alarm upon seeing so many refugees stream into the area.

Native American attacks on isolated farms continued throughout much of 1757, a year in which Elias Brunner may have begun building the stone house called Schifferstadt. In June of that year, a panic swept the region when, as Maryland Governor Sharpe wrote, "a large Body of French & Indians were actually on their march from Fort Du Quesne towards our Frontiers with a great number of Waggons & some Artillery." An attack in the area of present day Emmitsburg, just 16 miles north of Frederick

Town, was reported in July.[21] In response, Sharpe called out 500 militiamen.[22]

This is probably when members of the Brunner family joined the fight. We surmise this from a muster roll. Though not dated, it survives in the manuscript collection of the Maryland Historical Society. Among the names are those of Joseph's sons Elias and John as well as John, Jr. Also listed are Stephen Ransberger, husband of Joseph's daughter Maria Cathrina and three Getzendanners, apparently sons of Christian Getzendanner, husband of Joseph's older daughter, Anna Barbara. Stephen was Elias's brother-in-law. Jacob, Adam and Balser Getzendanner, despite variant spellings in the record, were Elias's nephews. Adam Ramsberger was Stephen's son. The lists of names were submitted to the Committee on Accounts of the General Assembly of Maryland.[23]

Elias and Stephen were officers of the unit, being listed on the muster roll, respectively, as "Sergt." and "Capt." One of the duties of the Frederick County militia was to go to Fort Frederick and, as it were, hold down the fort whenever the regular troops were sent out on campaigns. The militia also patrolled the region around the fort.

Although the muster roll is not dated, it names men in the unit mentioned in Governor Sharpe's letter to Governor Dinwiddie of Virginia on August 10, 1757: "the Convoy that was sent to Fort Cumberland is returned without having seen an Enemy but soon after they left Fort Frederick some Mischief was done on our Frontiers which obligated me to order two small Detachments from the Militia to patrol for some time beyond our Settlements."[24]

Not all Indian groups fought against the British and American side. Some were British allies, especially the Cherokees with whom Maryland officials had negotiated a treaty in 1757. In May of that year the Cherokees vowed to avenge deaths of the English,[25] and the following month, 200 Cherokees went to war against the French.[26] At the same time, members of the Catawba tribe were reported to have defended settlers near Fort Cumberland from attacks by the Shawnee.[27]

Near the end of 1757, as the war continued in and around the region, members of the Brunner family were pulled further into the conflict, even as other settlers resisted getting involved. According to a letter from, Captain Alexander Beall to Governor Sharpe, the captain visited Frederick Town hoping to obtain wagons and horses for a convoy of supplies headed west to Fort Cumberland. The way this event played out strongly suggests that the residents of Frederick Town were never paid for their earlier cooperation with the war effort. As a result, people were not inclined to help again. No doubt they remembered how the army had mistreated their animals in earlier phases of the war.

Captain Beall wrote in his letter that he has had "wretched luck" in getting wagons to carry a "Supply of Provisions to Fort Cumberland." Upon arriving in Frederick Town on Wednesday, November 23rd, Beall asked the Sheriff for help, but he did not receive it. On Friday, Saturday and Sunday, Beall tried again to obtain horses and wagons, again without success. By Sunday evening, he realized that "most of the People who lived in Town employed themselves … in Secreting their Waggons and Horses." Several more attempts were made to take people's possessions, all foiled by the locals. But then, as Beall writes, "some of the leading Dutch [Germans], Shellman, Bruner and others agreed to get the farmers together and that they should get the quantity [of horses and wagons] wanted."

Then the townsfolk raised a new concern. If their equipment were taken out of Maryland, across the Potomac and into the independent province of Virginia, they might not be eligible for remuneration. After all, in the past Frederick residents had not been paid for goods they had supplied to the Army, even though their requests were submitted to the Assembly and the Governor. Hoping to improve his luck, Beall asked for help from a prominent member of the local community—Capt. Stephen Runsburgh—"but the People continued still Clamorous and insisting on my paying according to Valuation or giving Security … and with many threats declared no waggons should be carried out of Town."

Some settlers dismantled their wagons before the British could take them. Some hid their wagons. Some set their horses loose. One man, Beall wrote, "cut out his horses in the middle [of the] Manococy River and rid [rode] off with them."

Then ensued one of the more dramatic and least known incidents in the war. When a detachment of British troops tried to take a particular group of horses, several women blocked the soldiers' path and, according to Beall, "stood by the Horses with long knives to prevent the Soldiers coming near them." After a standoff, the soldiers retreated. No less than the men, the women of Frederick Town were prepared to fight for their rights.

The following Wednesday, "Capt. Runsburgh and some others came to Town and told me they had been out since six that morning and they could not get one Horse and that the people were all under Arms and bid them to tell me they would neither Obey the Governor nor any Body else and that they would sooner loose their lives than go on any such Service unless the Governor would appoint one in Town to pay them."

Unable to procure the equipment and supplies he needed, Beall was forced to leave Frederick Town with only a few horses and bags, in which to transport supplies.[28]

Aside from what these incidents say about the attitude of Frederick County settlers toward the war, they show that the Brunner and Ramsburg families had become leaders in the German community. This description also suggests that a clear division existed between the British authorities and German settlers. Because Stephen Ramsburg is referred to as Captain, his rank undoubtedly placed him in the middle of this situation. Moreover, the fact that he was a wheelwright meant he would have known the owners of many wagons and where to find them.[29]

Presumably many, if not all, residents had taken the Oath of Allegiance to the British Crown when they sailed into American ports. It is striking then that they were uncooperative with British officers, even to the point of hostility. Considering the devastating effect of King Louis XIV's wars on their homeland, one would expect the Germans to align themselves with enemies of the French. But there was another factor. Britain, in trying to push the borders of Pennsylvania into the Ohio Valley, was guilty of the same kind of territorial aggression they had known in the old country. And by aiding the British, "they would seem only to be aiding the other provinces to expand their territory."[30] The Germans were not of a mind to support rulers bent on territorial expansion.

Despite the war's turmoil, life not only continued apace in Frederick

Town, the Brunners in particular were gradually improving their lives. In 1758 as hostilities were raging, Elias built a fine, stone home on the land that his father had named Schifferstadt. (The house and its people are the subject of Chapters 10, 11 and 12.)

Palatine settlers had been streaming into Frederick County since the 1730s. They had worked hard to transform the wilderness into cultivated farmland, not unlike what their forebears had done in the Rhine Valley. Some, like the Brunners, had been able to purchase their land and by the early 1750s, had achieved a level of prosperity. Their annual payments of quit-rents and taxes enriched their landlord, Daniel Dulany, and, in turn, financed Lord Baltimore's extravagant life back in England—facts that must have grated on the Germans. In return, the Maryland Assembly, other than funding the construction of Fort Frederick and a monetary payment to Indians on the British side, repeatedly failed to appropriate enough money to defend the frontier.

Therefore, it seems likely that the attitude of the self-sufficient Germans of Frederick County was to protect their own survival by refusing to supply the British Army unless they were certain of reimbursement.

Compensation from the British authorities was also deficient when it came to paying the militiamen, all of whom had stepped away from their farms for periods of weeks or months at a time and, as a result, sustained economic losses. Many militiamen waited almost ten years before receiving the pay that had been promised. When it finally came, many turned over their meagre pay to Captain Ramsburg.[31] This is a curious development, and the reason remains unknown. It is conceivable that Ramsburg, a wheelwright, may well have helped replace wagons taken by the British army and did so on credit.

The French and Indian War ended in 1763 with the signing of the Treaty of Paris, in which France yielded to Britain its claims to territories east of the Mississippi River. But the war's effect on settlers did not end. Many came to realize that they were not as isolated and free as they had thought. Foreign powers could threaten their livelihoods and their peace. Thus, the ensuing years were a turning point in the attitude of Marylanders toward British loyalist rulers in the Assembly. Class distinctions were dividing people still further.

"Maryland's politicians were mostly men of wealth, men of breeding, men of the established [Anglican] church," historian David Curtis Skaggs wrote. But "this gentry leadership was not solving the economic and social problems of the colony."[32] Many of Frederick County's pioneers had been farmers from German lands and remembered well their oppression under aristocracy. No doubt they were unaware that they were nurturing the seeds of a Revolution to come.

9

Brunners on the Record, Part 2

Life in Frederick County could sometimes be disturbing quite aside from the war then winding down on the frontier. On the evening of April 13, 1762, for example, a 65-year-old German man named Uriah Wirt was traveling with his son from Virginia to Frederick Town. Just after sunset and about seven miles from town, according to the *Maryland Gazette*, one of the oldest newspapers in America (and still publishing), they were approached by a man on horseback who demanded their money. Then "almost at the same instant" fired his pistol. Wirt died within hours. His assailant, an Englishman identified as Richard Crosby, was soon captured and jailed.[1]

At a trial just two weeks later both Elias Brunner and John Brunner served as jurors.[2] Crosby, who also went by the name of Richard Dew, was convicted of murder and sentenced to be hanged two weeks hence.[3] Justice was swift but, perhaps surprisingly in a court system dominated by Englishmen and in a trial of an Englishman, Germans were put on the jury. Not only were Germans trusted by the English establishment, some clearly had a good command of the English language.

The years after the French and Indian War were relatively peaceful, but tensions were rising between English colonists and the British government in London. Members of the German community, including the Brunner family, eventually would become involved.

The stresses arose because Britain's expenses in that war were so great that Parliament felt American colonists should bear most of the cost. After all British troops were defending the colonists. Parliament enacted several taxes including the notorious 1765 Stamp Act, requiring that colonists buy a stamp to put on every piece of paper sold or issued by a government agency. Stamps were required on such things as newspapers, playing cards and pamphlets. Eventually the British government also imposed a tax on tea imported to the colonies.[4]

Colonists, who had no representatives in Parliament, fumed, coining the phrase "no taxation without representation."

The first place in America to formally repudiate the Stamp Act was Frederick County. It was the first official opposition to the notorious law by any unit of American government. On November 23, 1765, twelve Frederick County judges, today known in Maryland as the "Twelve Immortals," unanimously resolved that "all proceedings shall be valid and effectual without the use of Stamps."[5]

In the court session during which the Stamp Act was repudiated, John Brunner was serving as a grand juror.[6] It is not clear whether he was directly involved, but records show that he was serving in the court on that day. This John may have been the son of the patriarch, Joseph, or he may have been the son of that John or, perhaps, one of John's nephews bearing the same name.

A week later, on November 30, Fredericktonians staged a mock funeral for the Stamp Act wherein a copy of the law and an effigy of

Instead of displaying the required stamp on each copy of his newspaper, Jonas Green, publisher of the *Maryland Gazette,* joined many other publishers and printed this to show his displeasure and refusal to comply with the Stamp Act. Green suspended publication of the paper on Oct. 31, 1765 in protest of the Stamp Act and resumed on Jan. 30, 1766. The Stamp Act was repealed in March of that year.

the stamp distributor, Zachariah Hood, were buried in a coffin.[7] That happened on a Saturday, the weekly market day, and the Brunners likely were in town and witnessed the spectacle. The event is still celebrated in Frederick County as Repudiation Day.

Although tensions throughout the colonies were growing, it would be eight more years before the event transpired that won a larger place in history—the Boston Tea Party in 1773. The American Revolution was coming, but even then, most English colonists were not looking to break away from Britain. They hoped simply to persuade Parliament to be less oppressive. The Germans, having no ancestral ties to Britain and, having realized by this time that they were still subject to an autocratic government, were prepared to join the resistance.[8] In 1774 members of the Brunner family would again step away from their normal lives and get involved in military action.

It happened just after the Boston Tea Party when an outraged Parliament reacted by passing a series of punitive restrictions on Massachusetts, hoping to teach the colony a lesson and bring it into submission. The effect was just the opposite. The British called the new laws the Coercive Acts, but Americans up and down the Atlantic coast called them the Intolerable Acts. They began to feel that the separate colonies could soon share the fate of Massachusetts. There was a new feeling that all the colonies were involved in a common cause.

In September 1774, delegates from twelve of the thirteen colonies met in Philadelphia and formed the first Continental Congress, creating a shadow government in defiance of the British governors installed by Parliament. Among Congress's many acts was to call for an embargo on all trade with Britain. To enforce that action, Congress called for the creation of committees of men in each city and county who were to keep an eye on trade in their area and look for violations of the embargo. These groups were variously called committees of inspection or committees of observation. The committee in Frederick County was chaired by John Hanson, who would become a delegate to the Congress and be elected its first president.[9]

On November 18, 1774, two members of the Brunner family were named to the Frederick County committee. One was an Elias Bruner, spelled in the record with one "n," who could be either the Elias who built Schifferstadt or the Elias who was a son of Jacob Brunner, a brother of Elias. The other committee member was John Remsburg, son of Stephen Remsburg.[10] There is no record of what actions these men may have taken. In some cases, violators' names were merely published in official newspapers. In others contraband merchandise was destroyed.

Within months the towns of Lexington and Concord, just outside Boston, saw the first gun battle of the American Revolution, which Ralph Waldo Emerson memorably called the "shot heard 'round the world." In the summer of 1775, the Continental Congress called upon each colony to raise militias. Annapolis assigned Frederick the responsibility of forming eight companies. Hundreds of Frederick County men signed up including Jacob Brunner,[11] probably a grandson of patriarch Joseph, and Valentine Brunner, another grandson.[12]

As the war unfolded over the next few years, Frederick County became a major supplier of grain, especially wheat, to George Washington's army. Wheat was the chief cash crop of German farmers. (For themselves they preferred rye.) The price of wheat soared, and it seems likely that the Brunners did what many others did—expand production and make more money.[13]

After the British surrendered at Yorktown in 1781, ending hostilities, the German settlers of Frederick were joined by other Germans, mercenary soldiers brought to America by the British to fight on their side, but now prisoners of war. Known as Hessians, thousands had come from the German province of Hesse. Many were sent to Frederick and housed in the building known today as the Hessian Barracks.[14] It is on the campus of the Maryland School for the Deaf in Frederick City.

German prisoners remained a prominent element in the town's life for two more years—up to the war's official end in 1783. German settlers naturally recognized a kinship, at least in language, with the prisoners. In fact, some escaped Hessians met up with local women and started families. Eventually the Continental Congress ordered that German prisoners who had married American women be freed after paying a fee.[15]

The war's end prompted exuberant celebrations across the new country. Perhaps the best description of festivities in Frederick Town was offered by one of the freed Hessian soldiers, Johann Conrad Döhla. In his diary he wrote (as translated):

Thereupon a peace-celebration bonfire was built by the regular troops and the militiamen stationed here, and they paraded behind the resounding sounds of fifes and drums through all of the streets and ways of this place with white flags, green caps, and laurel wreaths on their heads, and firing their weapons. With each volley, old and young gave an extraordinarily loud cheer: "Hyroh for peace! Hyroh for the liberty! Hyroh for Washington! Hyroh for Congress! For Hancock! [presumably John Hancock, he of the large signature on the Declaration of Independence] *For ourselves! God save the General Washington, our Master!" An 18-pound cannon was brought here also, and this was fired more than thirty times from a height before the city.*

At night a beautiful fireworks display took place, which was pre-pared for the Americans by our Artillery Captain [Nikolaus Friedrich] Hoffman and his artificers and cannoneers, for pay. It was very beautiful to see.[16]

By this time Elias Brunner had sold Schifferstadt and moved into town, so he very likely witnessed or even participated in the spectacle. His brothers who might still be on their farms, which were adjacent to Schifferstadt, may either have come into town to join the celebration, or watched the rockets from just a mile away.

The war made the American colonies independent of Great Britain, but despite creating a "perpetual union" it did not really create a new country.[17] In effect it created thirteen little countries independent of Great Britain. There was no real national government. That would have to wait for the Constitutional Convention of 1787, which laid down the framework for the government we know today.

The years immediately after the war were times of peace but not of plenty. European countries had reduced or cut off trade with America. The colonies had run up deep debts to pay for the war. Prices of general commodities rose. A recession set in.

The grain-based economy of Frederick County, which had boomed to supply the war effort, collapsed and with it, no doubt, the fortunes of the

The Conestoga wagon, developed by German settlers in
Pennsylvania, was the chief freight hauler of its day.
Larger ones were pulled by six horses.

Brunners. But by the 1790s, it seems to have been growing again. In 1791, for example, the county had 80 grist mills. Additionally, between 300 and 400 stills were recorded, along with 47 tanners, two glass works, two iron forges and two paper mills.[18]

Indeed, in 1791 a Polish writer traveled through Frederick County and was impressed by the region's abundance. Julian Ursyn Niemcewicz described the land as a "countryside both well cultivated and bountiful. Except for forest regions which were not extensive but occurred more often, the eye everywhere sees tremendous tracts of all sorts of grain. Great farm wagons harnessed to six horses were carrying flour and goods to and fro, and filled the fields and woods with sound of horse bells as they plodded slowly along."[19] A fair share of that abundant grain surely came from the large fields of the Brunners who were still farming.

By 1797 Frederick Town had more than 449 houses.[20]

Starting long before the Revolutionary War, there was a darker side to the Brunner family's lives. Two brothers left wills that tell us they held other human beings in bondage. Henry, the third son of Joseph and Cathrina, owned a man whom we know only as Samuel. Henry's will specifies that his son, also a Henry, is to have "fifty pounds aforehand or my Negro Samuel." Either way, the will says, "fifteen years after this Date my Negro Samuel is to be free." The will was executed in 1776, so if Samuel survived, he would have been freed in 1791.[21]

John Brunner, second son of Joseph and Cathrina, owned four people. In John's will two, named Fortune and Will, were bequeathed to one son while two others, named Nat and Sal, went to another son "with their increase." That appears to be a reference to their children. None are given last names. There is no hint that these four people would ever be free.[22]

Elias Brunner, the builder of Schifferstadt's stone house, appears not to have had slaves, at least not when he made out his will. It makes no mention of slaves. That could be because he had left the family farm twelve years earlier and moved into downtown Frederick where he may have had no need of slaves. He died in 1783.[23] No wills for other Brunners of the first or second generation have turned up, leaving open the question of whether they owned slaves.

One way or the other, however, there is no question that all European settlers benefitted from the pernicious institution. Maryland was a slave state, and slave labor contributed mightily to the growing affluence of the entire white population.

Court records show further minor transactions by other Brunners, Ramsburgs and other variants of those names. All those families did, of course, grow and become founders and builders of Frederick County.

As the newborn United States began to face the world, the Brunner family—now Americans in every sense—might have looked back on the extraordinary journey that had brought them to their new lives. But the horrors of their old lives and the travails of their ocean passage were fast fading into the past. Indeed, the younger generation—the grandchildren of Joseph and Cathrina—surely could not remember any life other than in Pennsylvania and then Maryland. Nor could they imagine how the family's legacy, including a large and fine stone house still bearing the name of the family's hometown in Germany, would be treasured in 21st century America.

10

A Year at Schifferstadt

What follows is a fictionalized account of life at Schifferstadt in the 1760s after the stone house was built and the turmoil of the French and Indian War had ended. This portrayal is based on historical evidence of life on Elias and Albertina Brunner's farm, including their home, which still exists. And it is based on common practices among German settlers in Frederick County in those days.

SPRING

It's a fine warm day at Schifferstadt, and the pace of life is quickening. Mother cleans the breakfast dishes and tells the children that she saw an oriole in the apple trees, a sure sign of the coming season. It was hopping among the new, light-green leaves, she says, probably looking for insects or tasty flower buds. Mother opens the kitchen windows to let in fresh air and sends the young ones down to the cellar to see if any turnips have survived the winter.

Stephan, the 10-year-old, takes a candle down the ladder because it's dark under the barrel-vaulted ceiling with only a little outside light coming through the two vents. Peter, four years younger, follows. They are struck by how cold it is even as the outside air feels so warm these days. The last three good turnips are going into the pot for supper.

Mother steps from the cutting table to the fireplace and pulls her petticoat out of the way as she heaps red-hot coals at one side of the broad fireplace. Then she links two segments of iron hangers to suspend the cast-iron pot above the heat. It will simmer gently until mealtime.

Father decided earlier this morning that winter is finally over. So he put his woolen trousers into a bedroom chest and brought out his linen trousers. Ready for nicer weather, he sits in a chair by the kitchen window, looking to the east, past the barn. He finishes his coffee as he waits for the sun to get a little higher. Soon enough he puts on his hat and walks out to the upper field to check on the wheat and rye. He and the boys sowed them late last summer.[1] The seeds sprouted then and grew into lovely carpets of green.

When winter came, the little wheat and rye plants went dormant. Only now that the air is warming have they resumed growing. There looks to be a fairly thick stand of each. Seems like the crows didn't take too much seed when it fell on the ground, and they haven't pulled up many of the seedlings. Father walks back to the house and reports this to Mother. He has another piece of dark bread slathered with butter. Some of last year's rye went into the bread and some is being saved in a bag in the attic to be malted (sprouted), fermented and distilled for whiskey. Mother rinses the turnips in a bowl of water, pours it into the sink and watches the muddy water flow under the window sill and outside into a wooden bucket just below the sink's spout. Later, this water will go into the garden if it's dry.

Then Father heads out again, walking about five minutes to the lower field far behind the house, crossing Carroll's Creek on carefully placed stepping stones. He wants to see if the soil is still too wet to plow. It is, and that's not good. This year's corn, a crop Germans have just started growing, mainly for animal feed, needs to get into the ground soon, and that can't happen until the field is plowed and then harrowed, using an implement that rakes the soil smooth. Skilled farmers don't plant corn in the same fields two years in a row. Oats need to go in soon, too.

There is plenty of work to do. The ewes were bred last fall and should start lambing quite soon. Father and the boys have already prepared little pens in the barn, covered with clean wheat straw from last summer's harvest.

Back at the house Mother reminds six-year-old Peter to feed the chickens and to gather eggs. Stephan already knows it's his job to milk the cow every morning. Mother does it in the afternoon, making sure to strip every drop. The children march to the hen house and the barn, one swinging the egg basket, the other a milk pail. The barn is made mostly of stone but includes an older log section that Father and Grandfather built shortly after settling on this land more than 20 years ago. All together it's a little larger than the house and as solidly built. It stands just beyond the front driveway.

The house sits empty as Mother goes out to the barn to get an iron hoe and a wooden rake to prepare the kitchen garden for spring planting. The family's fresh vegetables depend heavily on her plot just beyond the back door—all laid out in the traditional four neat squares of raised beds enclosed by a larger square, all of it surrounded by a fence. At the center where the four smaller squares meet is a yucca plant, its hardy, swordlike leaves having stood guard all winter.[2]

Mother opens the gate, enters and closes it carefully behind her. She needs to be careful because the hinges are rusting out even though Father paints them with linseed oil every year, the oil pressed from some of their flax seeds at the oil mill. The picket fence, about four feet high, keeps out hungry rabbits, woodchucks and other marauders. The bison and elk, which once were common in these parts, retreated to the wilderness years ago. Deer can leap the fence easily, but if anybody spots one in time, Father will try to shoot it.

In a narrow bed that runs all the way around the garden and just inside the fence are perennial herbs such as bee balm, chamomile, sage and rosemary. They die down each winter but come back faithfully every spring. Nearest the gate is "thunder weed," a perennial sedum that German settlers swear protects the house from lightning strikes. It has worked so far.

The raised beds, edged with wooden boards that hold soil well above the paths, mean that the soil drains quickly and warms up earlier, even as Father's lower field stays too wet. That's why he was able to turn the soil in Mother's garden a few days ago with a spade. Now she needs to break up the big clods with her hoe and rake the beds smooth.

All the soil is clean, not a weed in sight. Along the edge of one bed there is a tangle of twigs and brown tree leaves. Underneath that protective cover are a few lettuce plants that struggled through the winter and are putting up new leaves. A lettuce salad, wilted by hot bacon grease, will be most welcome after a winter of aging vegetables and grains.

Just as Mother starts to pull the leaves aside to check on the lettuce, she hears a scream from the barn.

"Mama! Mama! Hurry!"

Mother drops what she's doing and races around the house to the barn.

"Here!" both boys call.

It's the lambing pen and one of the ewes has dropped a new addition to the family flock. The boys stare, reminded of how life works. Mother is pleased that there will be more wool for the winter clothing. Two more ewes are in the pen, bellies bulging with promise.

Is that all the eggs you found? Mother asks Peter. He trudges back to the hen house, next to the barn. In fact, it's so early in the spring that the hens aren't laying much yet. And Stephan's bucket shows that he didn't finish milking. Finally, Stephan takes the milk to the cellar and sets it in the niche at the far end. There it will cool down, the cream floating to the top. In a few days one of the children will churn the cream into butter.

Mother walks back to her garden, slowing down as she passes the apple trees to see if the oriole is still looking for insects. She picks up her tools and hoes a patch in one of the squares, then rakes it smooth. Now she is ready to make an investment in summer's meals. She reaches into her apron for a small piece of old linen wrapped around a handful of tiny, black onion seeds saved from last year's plants. Carefully she unfolds it, whispers "In the name of God," and trickles the seeds into perfectly straight furrows scratched into the ground.[3] Gently her fingers brush soil over the seeds and pat it down.

In another part of the kitchen garden Mother plants peas in a wide patch. They'll vine up the little forest of sticks and tree branches she has stuck into the ground. In a few weeks there will be fresh peas to eat right away. It's a delicacy she learned from an English neighbor. In a much larger area near the pasture, Father will plant the regular field peas to be dried and saved in the attic for winter.

That's only the start of the garden. Good Friday comes in a few days, and as every God-fearing German of the countryside knows, that's the day to sow seeds of cabbage and flowers.[4] Ancient gardening wisdom is not to be ignored. Mother hoes and rakes more patches to be ready for that auspicious day. In front of the house, she does the same, getting ready to plant bachelor's buttons, whose blue flowers look pretty against the gray stone of the house, and remind her of the flax blossoms that should start appearing in June. She prepares beds for hollyhocks flanking the front door.

Over the next few days in the four-square garden, Mother and her young helpers will plant savoy cabbage, carrots, parsnips, peppers, cucumbers and root parsley. She plants green beans on poles as tall as she is. The boys ask her to save a patch for popcorn, a crop developed by the Indians and a treat every European settler has come to enjoy.

Father, too, is getting ready to plant. On the 100th day of the year a proper German farmer will put in his potatoes, cabbages, tobacco and flax— all crops that like to start growing in cool weather. Some farmers counted days, some figured that April 1 was easier to remember and others went by the rule of planting flax when trees show the first tinge of green. Father thinks the trees are starting to green up and, in fact, the 100th day comes shortly. He has two good reasons to plow soon.[5]

He has been saving an area next to the upper field. The upper and lower fields together amount to about fifty acres, which is about as much as Father figures is needed to sustain the family and to grow extra to sell. Of course, no farm grows everything it needs; every farm grows or makes products to sell or trade for other things it must have. The soil is still as rich and tillable as when Grandfather and Grandmother chose this place and settled here. That's because when any one area begins to yield less, usually after three or four years, Father lets it lie fallow for several years and moves to a field that has recovered its fertility. Sometimes he sows clover in the fallow field, a miracle plant that makes the soil richer. In summer he may cut the tall grasses for hay. The horses, sheep and cattle graze on pasture and, of course, deliver their own fertilizer.

Father's older brother, who lives at the neighboring farm, is experimenting with turnips to enrich exhausted soil. He sows turnip seed and feeds some of the plants, including their bulbous roots, to his cattle but leaves most in the soil to die down, decay and eventually be plowed in. If it seems worth the cost of the seed, Father might try it next year.

Back at the barn Father climbs over the fence, and into a small paddock to check on the family's pair of tall, heavy Conestoga horses. It's a strong, sturdy breed developed by the Germans in Pennsylvania. Father's pair are descendants of the animals that Grandfather and Grandmother used to pull their wagons from Lancaster County when they first moved to Maryland all those years ago.

Yesterday Father rounded them up from somewhere behind the house where they usually roam free, feeding mostly on wild grass that grows along the creek. The pair always stay together and seldom roam far from the corn that Father offers at the barn. The cattle and hogs, which also roam free, are marked with a specific pattern of slits and cropped ears. Each farmer has his own pattern of earmarks or brands burned into the skin recorded at the courthouse, in case any disputes arise.[6]

Next Father checks the wooden plow. He made it last year from a carefully chosen chestnut board with fine, closely-spaced grain. He sawed it, chiseled it, shaped it with an adze. When held at the correct angle, the plow's thin forward edge can slice into the soil a few inches down and force the uplifted soil up until it flips over to the left. To that so-called moldboard Father had attached a long wooden pole that reaches forward between the horses and attaches to their collars. Two wooden handles reach back from the moldboard so that Father can grasp them. It's an ancient design, little changed in thousands of years, and it gets the job done, although a wooden plow barely lasts two seasons.

Father calls Stephan. At ten, he's already had a few years of experience guiding the horses. Father hitches up the team as Stephan lifts the plow into a small cart. The two farmers head to the lower field, which has had time to dry out. Father leads the horses and Stephan pulls the cart.

At the field, the plow is set on the ground and hitched to the horses. Now Stephan leads the horses as Father muscles the plow, keeping its leading edge angled into the soil but not more than four or five inches or it will dig in too far and jam. An arrow-straight furrow releases the warm, rich smell of brown earth, as sure a sign of spring as Mother's oriole. After a while, Father takes a rest and lets Stephan try his hand at the plow.

When the plowing is done, Father will bring out the harrow—a framework of logs with many wooden teeth pointing down. As the horse drags it across the plowed field, it combs the soil into a smoother surface, making it ready for planting. Some farmers have switched to iron teeth, and Father is saving up to buy some from the blacksmith.

When Good Friday rolls around Mother and Peter sow her flower seeds, and Father plants cabbage seeds in part of the large plot that he and Stephan plowed and harrowed a few days earlier. Those things done, the family refrains from gardening or plowing for three days because, as everyone knows, Jesus lay buried until Easter. After that one could resume working the soil. April 10, the 100th day of the year, will be especially busy. When it comes time, Stephan sets the cut-up "seed" potatoes in a shallow trench that Father plowed near the cabbage patch. Then Father and Stephan fork manure into the trench and rake the soil to cover them.

This is also the time to put in spring barley, which will be ready by late summer, and the all-important flax. According to the old rule of thumb, it takes a quarter-acre of flax to yield enough linen for a year's worth of clothing for each member of the family. Flax should be planted as early as the soil can be plowed, and it's getting a little late.[7]

When the day is right, Father and Mother go up to the attic where sacks of last year's grain are stored. They hang large hemp bags around their necks and fill them with seed, sometimes barley and sometimes wheat. It's the same grain Mother might cook for a meal, but she is always careful to save enough to use as seed. When planted each bushel of seed can yield ten bushels of harvested grain—if the rains are good. Mother and Father head out to a field and, walking at a steady pace, take handfuls of seed and sow them, rhythmically swinging their arms left and right as they broadcast seed over the ground. The idea is to distribute the seed evenly. Too close together and the seedlings will stunt one another; too far apart and some of the prepared field is wasted. Another trip over the field with the harrow buries the seeds.

Pound for pound tobacco is the most valuable crop a settler can grow, and some farmers choose to put in a little. If you don't smoke it yourself, you can take the dried leaves to a tobacco warehouse and receive a note that is as good as cash in local stores.[8] In fact, the value of money is often stated as its equivalent in pounds of tobacco.

But raising that crop takes the effort of everyone in the family. A few weeks earlier Father had broadcast the tiny seeds in a small patch. Now the seedlings are a few inches tall. In May the whole family will transplant them into rows in a larger field. That's a job for Father and both boys.

Twice a week from then on, the boys must kneel or bend over each tobacco plant and examine each leaf for worms, which can defoliate a plant in days and happen to be exactly the same color as the leaves. The boys pick off the worms and crush them on the spot. Father reminds them to look on each leaf's underside for eggs laid by the adult tobacco moth. Those must be crushed too. When she has time, Mother checks the tobacco plants as well.[9]

Mother's time is especially limited when she makes soap. For months she has been saving chunks of animal fat, bacon rinds and grease from cooking. And Stephan has been saving ashes from the fireplaces to make lye. You need the unlikely combination of both to make a product that gets things clean, and doing it demands Mother's sense of practical chemistry. Both operations are done outdoors whenever enough raw materials have been saved up.

To make lye she uses a barrel with a spigot near the bottom. She stuffs a dense layer of straw and twigs at the bottom, fills the barrel with ashes and slowly pours jugs of water over it. As the water trickles down, it extracts caustic compounds from the ashes and flows out the spigot into an iron kettle.

To prepare the fat, she boils the saved grease and chunks of fat for hours, rendering the actual fat from the solids. The stench keeps Mother on the upwind side of the fire. Then she adds a quantity of water and boils the pot for hours more. When it's time to start supper, she lets the fire die down and leaves it for the night.

The next morning the various ingredients have separated. Pure fat has floated to the top of the water, and the solids have sunk below it. Mother scoops out the fat and mixes it in another pot with just the right amount of lye. Now she must boil the combination for hours more. Once the mixture has cooled, it is soft soap, which she calls *"schmier-seef"*, or "smear soap."[10]

At a shop in town she could buy hard soap, but it's exactly the same thing with a little salt thrown in to make it solidify. But that would mean wasting all the grease and ashes that are produced in the house anyway.

SUMMER

Life at Schifferstadt barely slows down in summer. Most of the crops are in the ground. The wheat and rye have turned into amber waves of grain. They'll be ready to harvest soon.

The flax will bloom in June, and Mother always says the field of blue flowers looks like a reflection of the sky. The plants will stand in the field until the leaves start to turn yellow. The hemp, always seeded so close together that the plants shoot upward to compete for light, is taller than Father and on its way to being still taller.

Of course, the boys still must milk the cow and gather eggs every day. And Mother cooks every meal every day, sometimes with help from the hired girl. She's the 14-year-old daughter of a family in Frederick Town. The Schifferstadt family in these years is unusual in having no daughter of their own. The girl does most of the cleaning in the house. She sleeps in one of the upstairs bedrooms, and the boys share the other. Mother is teaching her the cooking and housekeeping skills every woman needs to know to be a good wife.

One Saturday morning the boys wolf down their breakfast and so does the hired girl. Every Saturday is market day in a town that has grown to nearly 200 homes and shops as well as two churches, one German and one English. Frederick Town has just about everything a person could want. It has blacksmiths, brick makers, wagon makers, weavers, millers, tanners, gunsmiths, potters and coopers. For those who don't make their own clothing, which includes many town people, there are hatters, tailors and shoemakers. And there are many taverns and inns.[11] And best of all on market day, there will be lots of people including children from town and other farms. The hired girl will spend the day with her family. But the main purpose is buying and selling the goods people bring for sale.

It's an outdoor market on a large, grassy lot at the Market Space just off Market Street and between Church and Second streets. There are plans to build an indoor marketplace on the site. Frederick Town is growing so fast that some dealers want to have permanent stalls.

Today Mother needs to buy sugar, salt, coffee and a few other things. And she figures she might be able to pay for it all after selling the four pairs of men's long stockings that she knitted last winter. Also she has a basket of eggs to sell. Last week Mother's cheese had reached a degree of ripeness that she judged good, so she took it from the cellar and sold every bit of it.

Father hitches a horse to the wagon, and everybody climbs aboard, Mother and Father riding on the bench up front. It's only a mile to town, but there are heavy things to carry each way. When they reach the grassy market square, Stephan ties the horse to a hitching post and drags two wooden barrels off the wagon, a big hogshead and a smaller keg called a firkin. He and Peter roll them to an empty spot in the square. Mother sets a wide plank across the hogshead and arranges her stockings and egg basket on it. She has barely taken a seat on the firkin and adjusted her bonnet to keep the sun off her face before the boys race off. They join other boys already rolling iron or wood hoops from old barrels across the grass. Stephan and

Peter have brought their own hoops and are soon in races to see who can cross the grass fastest without losing the hoop. They ignore the girls who watch them from a distance.

Others from the surrounding area are also selling produce from their farms. There are stacks of carrots, bundles of spinach, heaps of potatoes, neat rows of early cabbages, baskets of strawberries and huckleberries. Two women have brought balls and skeins of yarn spun from their wool. The blacksmith's shop is next to the marketplace, and he always displays his wares out front. Father wants a pair of new hinges for that garden gate that Mother has been complaining about, and he needs more nails for repairs around the place.

Haggling at the market, by Lewis Miller, an early 19th century
Pennsylvania German folk artist.
From the collection of the York County Heritage Trust, York, PA.
Used by permission.

Father wanders through the market, checking out the harness that a friend has made to sell. He casually examines a very fine calf that he might want to buy to join the milk cow that is getting on in years. But he tries not to show too much interest just yet.

Most people speak German, of course. These are friends and neighbors, most of them having come from the same part of the old country and having spent time in Pennsylvania first. Sometimes they reminisce about the old days, but most often talk turns to the weather and how the crops are coming along. Is Herr Bentz still growing so much tobacco despite the price drop? And Frau Ransbergerin, is she here with her delicious schmalzkuchen? Father usually likes to buy some of those doughnuts to take home.

After just a few hours, Mother has sold all her stockings and nearly all the eggs. She now has money to visit the grocer's shop, which fronts onto the marketplace and sells things people can't grow for themselves. In her pocket—a linen bag on a cloth belt under her petticoat—is paper money, a few shillings and pence. Not only are there commodities such as sugar and salt but tea leaves and coffee beans, pins and needles, ribbons, buttons, even broad-brimmed hats for the men. (Fancier hats that the English women wear are at the milliner's.)

As Mother enters the shop, a young black man, the grocer's apprentice, perhaps a slave, steps up and offers to help. Then ensues a conversation in which one party struggles in English and the other does his best in German. They understand one another well enough. The man tells her about some products that have just arrived—various spices and raisins. Mother is tempted. The man brings the items Mother wants and wraps them in paper. She reaches her pocket through a slit at the side of her petticoat.[12]

As the afternoon wears on Mother and Father find each other and load the groceries into the wagon. Father bought that calf after all, and he ties it to the back of the wagon. It can walk to its new home. He finds the firkin and the hogshead, rolls them to the wagon and hoists them aboard. Somehow Stephan and Peter know it is time to go, and they have wandered back to the wagon as well. The hired girl has arranged to stay overnight with her parents and says she will meet Mother and Father at church the next morning.

On Sunday morning the family gets ready for church, everybody dressing in their best clothes. This time they walk into town. They need to be there early because Father is an elder and has roles to play during the service. Grandfather was a founding member of the German Reformed Church in Frederick a generation ago. At that time the building was made of logs, but a few years ago the congregation grew too large, and it was replaced with a larger stone building fronting on Church Street. The old log building was sold to the schoolmaster, Herr Schley.

After church Father and some of the other elders gather to discuss church business. A perennial sore point is what they call a double taxation that the colonial government imposes on German congregations. Like every citizen of Maryland, the Germans are taxed to support the church decreed official by Lord Baltimore—the Church of England.[13] But the Germans also had to pay the costs of building and maintaining their own church, which is now a fine, new building with what, when completed, will have the first spire in Frederick Town.[14]

While the elders talk, Mother chats with some of the women about plans for what they might bring to sell at the next market day. The boys run about, aimlessly it seems. The hired girl says she will walk back to Schifferstadt before dark. Sunday is her day off.

As summer wears on it's time again for serious work. Both rye and wheat need to be harvested, jobs that put the entire family in the field. Two of Father's brothers come over from their neighboring farms to help. They bring two of their slaves as well. Some German settlers refuse to own slaves, but others do have a few, generally from one to four. One brother has already decided to set his lone slave free when he dies. The other brother has not. Next week Father will help the brothers and their slaves harvest their crops.

As the men swing scythes, slicing stems close to the ground, the boys follow behind to pick up armloads of stalks heavy with heads of grain. Hugging as big a bundle as they can manage, the boys carry them to Mother, who takes one stalk and uses it to tie the others into a sheaf. Every so often she gathers four or five sheaves and leans them against one another, seed heads high, to make little teepees called shocks. There they will dry for a few days before being taken to the barn.

After a few days, if there has been no rain and the heads of rye and wheat have dried, the family heads back to the field with the big wagon, pulled by one of the horses. Everybody gathers sheaves and puts them in the wagon to be hauled to the barn. There the grain will stay dry until there is time to thresh, usually not till fall or winter. There's just too much work to do in the fields and in Mother's kitchen garden during the growing season.

Still, there is one old tradition that the boys remember well. If you want next year's harvest to be good, you must make and eat schmalzkuchen, those delicious confections that later Americans will call doughnuts. Mother obliges. And she remembers to save the lard in which they are deep fried to grease the wagon wheels. By tradition, it must be that same lard if you want to be able haul your grain to the mill.

Come July it's time to pull up the flax by the roots, a job for the whole family. Mother explains to the boys that it's important to get the full length of the stem and the roots. That way the filaments that she uses to make linen will be the longest and will make the strongest, smoothest thread.[15]

Stephan and Peter carry armloads of flax stems to the barn and pull the seed heads through coarse combs to separate the seeds. Some seeds will be saved for planting next year and some to be pressed for linseed oil. Then the boys carry the stems to a grassy field and spread them out. Over the next month or so, the morning dew and bacteria will weaken the outer skin and inner pith of the stems, turning them brittle, but leave the fibers intact, a process called retting. Eventually the boys load up a cart with the retted flax stems and haul them back to the barn. Now comes the real work— liberating the strong, pliable linen fibers from the dried husk that encloses each stem. Everybody pitches in, reenacting a series of steps that humans have carried out for thousands of years. To start, Stephen brings out a device called a brake and takes the first turn at it. He lifts its hinged wooden lever, lays a bundle of flax stems just under it and jams the lever down, chopping its two moveable, wooden bars between three fixed bars. Thus the stems are forced around sharp corners, shattering the brittle husks into bits. The two parts of the brake fit like oversized tongue-and-groove boards. The pliable fibers that will become linen remain undamaged.

After each lift of the lever, Stephan pulls the bunch of stems back to break a new section. He develops a rhythm, chopping with one arm and pulling with the other.

Flax plant, uprooted.

When his chopping arm aches, Peter takes over. Once a bundle of stems is broken, some clinging bits of husk must still be removed. Mother holds the bundle hanging next to a board for scutching. She beats it with what looks like a wooden knife. With each blow, she scrapes the knife down to force out the broken bits.

Then comes the hackling. Mother takes each bunch of stems—now limp linen fibers—and drags them through a fierce looking brush called a hackle, which some people call a hetchel. It's a forest of closely spaced, sharp nails driven up through a block of wood. Again and again, she pulls the bundle through, removing the short bits and combing the long ones into what looks like long, blonde human hair. In fact, blonde girls would often be said to have "flaxen hair." The short fibers that are combed out, called tow, are used to make twine and coarser fabrics such as tarps, towels and even ships' sails. Tow also makes good tinder for starting fires. A blond boy with unruly hair is sometimes called a tow head.

Every so often the family members, including the hired girl, rotate through each of the steps, putting the finished hanks of linen fiber into a basket that will go into the attic. There the fibers will stay until there is time in the winter to spin them into thread.

Come July, tassels atop the corn plants have finished shedding their pollen onto the silks below, so Father and the boys take knives to the field and slice off the top half of the stalks to use as fodder for livestock during the winter. Sometimes Father must reach above his head to cut the stalks, many of which are twice his height. Bundles of corn tops are tied into sheaves and set on the ground to dry for a day or two. Then they are loaded onto a wagon and hauled to the barn. At the barn Father stands in the wagon and pitches sheaves to Stephan and Peter in the loft. They do their best to catch the sheaves and walk them to the back of the loft, there to pile up and wait for winter. Corn leaves and stalks are highly nutritious for livestock.

In another field the hemp plants, which Father planted when he put in the flax, are stretching ever taller. Hemp makes excellent rope, and the taller the plant, the longer the fibers and the stronger the rope. Very soon the plants will be harvested and processed much like flax to get out the all-important fibers. As Father taught the boys, the trick to getting tall hemp plants is to drop the seeds close together. That way they compete for sunlight and put more of their energy into growing taller. The plants are taller than Father.

About once a week, starting in August if the weather is dry the boys go out to the tobacco patch to pick the oldest and biggest leaves, starting at the bottom where leaves have already reached full size. The leaves will be hung in the barn to dry. If the plant has begun to send up its flower spike, they cut the top off, forcing the plant to focus its growth on the remaining leaves. Of course, a few plants are left to flower and make seed for next year's crop. The boys weed around the plants with hoes.

German farmers take pride in keeping all their fields clean and tidy, each field surrounded by a well-maintained zig-zag fence of split rails, which the Germans call a worm fence. Father says you can always tell an English or Scots-Irish farm because their fields look weedy. Father always shakes his head when he sees how some of the English let their fields go.

Through the summer Mother has been going into the vegetable garden every morning to weed and see what might be ready to harvest. She kneels next to some gherkin cucumber vines, pulling a few small ones to make into pickles. The bigger cucumbers for fresh eating need a little more time to grow bigger.

In late summer, it's time for Mother to plant vegetables that like to grow into the cooler fall weather. Some even taste sweeter after a few frosts. She plants spinach, turnips, lettuce and chard. They go into the patch where the sweet spring peas finished weeks ago. Father's field peas finished as well but they're for winter eating. They were allowed to dry hard on the plants and then harvested, piled into baskets and bags and hauled up to the attic.

FALL

When the first cool days arrive, it's time to sow winter wheat and rye. But before that the dried ears of corn must be twisted off their stalks, loaded onto a cart and taken to the barn. Father grows his corn the traditional way—in clusters of stalks set two or three paces apart in each direction. That leaves just enough room for a horse-drawn cart to move between the stalks.

When the cart is full, Peter, now going on seven, leads the horse back to the barn and everybody unloads the ears onto the barn floor. When all the corn has been harvested some of the neighbors will come over for a shucking bee or, as some call it, a frolic. It's one of the few social events in a Maryland German's calendar, and it has the advantage of getting work done while bringing together whole families to share news and gossip as they separate the cobs from their dry husks. It's also a time for young people to socialize. The husks pile up on the floor as the yellow cobs go into baskets, which the men carry to the corn crib, a room of the barn enclosed by boards spaced to let air flow through. But shelling happens later, when there is time.

Now comes one of the activities that the boys enjoy most—making sauerkraut. They like it because they are the designated stompers. A

heap of cabbages waits in the kitchen. First each cabbage is sliced in half and slid repeatedly over the sharp blades of a shredder, or *Krauthobel*, that straddles a large crockery bowl on the kitchen table. The device is like a carpenter's plane turned upside down or the device later cooks will call a mandoline. Mother works the cabbage quickly, and once shreds fill the bowl, she dumps them into a new oak firkin. Father sprinkles salt on the cabbage.

Now the fun begins. Father lifts Peter and sets him inside the keg. Of course, he had already rolled up his trousers and washed his feet. Mother saw to that. Peter stomps up and down and turns a full circle, crushing the cabbage shreds until they are well bruised. By then Mother has another bowl of cabbage shreds. Peter is hoisted out to make room for the next layer of cabbage and a sprinkling of salt. Now Stephan is the stomper. He's big enough to step in by himself.

And so it goes, each layer of cabbage and salt being crushed just enough to squeeze out some of the juices. The stompers take turns. When the barrel is full Father pushes it out of the way to a corner of the kitchen near the ladder to the cellar. Mother sets a wooden disc on the shreds and weights it with a stone. Now it's just a matter of waiting while the magic happens. Nobody knew at the time, but natural bacteria on the cabbage leaves would ferment the vegetable juice and shreds, producing a crunchy and sour-salty flavor that every German family loved. They had no idea that it was rich in vitamin C.

Every day or so Mother checks the keg, watching as froth forms at the surface. She forks up a bit to taste. After a few weeks she judges it to be proper sauerkraut. Then Father and Stephan wrestle the firkin down to the cellar where the cold temperature will stop fermentation and preserve the kraut through most of the winter.[16]

Fall is also the time to harvest apples. Like every German farm, Schifferstadt has a large orchard with dozens of trees. For weeks, the boys have been testing the fruit for ripeness every few days, usually stopping just short of making themselves sick. But apples are mainly for making hard cider. Apples can be baked in pies or mashed and cooked into a rich, sweet apple butter. Perfect apples with no blemish or soft spot are packed in a barrel and stored in the cellar. As everybody knows, one rotten apple can spoil the barrel.

Father keeps some of the fermented cider to make into what the English call applejack. When freezing weather comes, he puts a crock of it outside. When ice forms on the surface, it's mostly water with little of the alcohol. Father tosses that away, leaving cider with more concentrated alcohol. Repeated cycles of freezing and discarding the ice, called jacking, further increase the alcohol content. A good, stiff drink of applejack comforts a body during the long winter nights.[17]

Before the weather gets that cold, though, some of the fresh apples need to be cored, peeled, sliced and either dried or boiled in a huge pot to make apple butter. As with the husking bee, this is a time for friends and family to gather. Baskets of apples are brought into the parlor with lots of crockery bowls and knives. People sit around a table, grab apples and start in. It's a schnitzing bee, schnitz (or snitz) being German for slice or carve. Some slices will be dried in a warm oven and stored in the attic for cooking later, either in pies or as sweet ingredients in other dishes. Others will be tossed into a pot simmering in the kitchen fireplace. Nothing goes to waste; the cores and peelings are hauled out to a feeding trough for the hogs.

Sometimes when work in the fields has slackened a bit, and the air has turned cool Father likes to go hunting, mainly in the fields and forests behind the house. Fall is a good time to get a fat turkey. Like almost every German farmer he owns a Pennsylvania long rifle, a fine piece invented by a German gunsmith back in the first province of America where the family lived when Father was a little boy. It's superior to the old English musket because it shoots straighter and farther. That's because of two things—the barrel, between five and six feet long, is much longer than a musket's, and the inside has spiraling grooves, called rifling, that set the ball spinning, which keeps it flying in a straighter path. In later years it would also be called a Kentucky rifle.[18]

Of course, the boys always want to go along, and Father always lets them. Stephen is already a fairly good shot. Peter has a ways to go, what with the rifle weighing close to ten pounds. If the hunters bag something, there will be fresh meat for supper.

As the calendar turns to late October, the family's excitement starts building toward one of the most enjoyable events of the year—the Fall market fair in town. It's a three-day event with food, music, entertainers, livestock competitions, horse races—all of it an escape from the work that dominates everyone's days for most of the year.[19] Just about everybody from miles around will be there. The militia will be mustering with their long rifles. There might even be acrobats; some came last year and put on a show.

Stephan is looking forward to the cudgeling competition. It's like a sword fight but with long sticks. He's been practicing his moves behind the woodshed and trying to get Peter to fight with him. He wants to enter the tournament. But Mother said no. Last year one of the neighbor boys got whacked so hard on the head that he was laid up for two days. Still Stephan wants to watch the others fight.

The family walks into town for the big event. This year there is an English language puppet show for children, called "Punch and Judy." An Englishman does the puppets, thrusting his hands above a tiny stage. Another man collects a small fee to watch it. The boys, already becoming bilingual, find it easy to understand the characters. One puppet always seems annoyed by the other and keeps whacking it with a little stick. Peter laughs every time, but Stephen soon finds it boring and wanders off to join some friends watching horse races.

Father likes to check out the livestock exhibits. Some of the farmers have brought in cattle or pigs that they're especially proud of. Father wonders whether his animals look as good as these. He decides they do and resolves to bring some of his best animals next year.

Mother is shopping for kitchenware. There's some really nice pottery, but it seems a bit expensive. Instead she stops at the tinsmith's booth and buys a lantern that holds a candle but has lots of holes in the metal sides. The holes are both decorative and let light shine out. It'll be good for carrying around the house at night and not having to move slowly.

Next to the tinsmith is Herr Dannwolf's stall. He's a glassmaker who lives just a few miles north of Schifferstadt. His factory is there, too.[20] He made the window glass in the house. Today he has brought several colorful bottles that he and his assistants have made. Two of the assistants are indentured servants from the Palatinate, the same area of Germany where Mother and Father were born. She tells the assistants that she left there as a little girl and doesn't remember much about it. They tell her that conditions in the old country are not much better and that they are happy to be in America, even though it means they still must work for Herr Dannwolf for two more years.

When the most urgent work on the farm is done, it's time to thresh the grain. The sheaves have been waiting since summer, heaped on the barn floor to one side of the big central doors. Just inside those doors is the wide threshing floor, a surface of wooden planks. It stretches from one doorway to another at the back of the barn. Father and the boys take armloads of wheat sheaves and spread them over the threshing floor, making a layer almost deep enough to bury a chicken. Each one takes a flail, an ancient tool consisting of two wooden sticks linked by a leather strap that loosely ties the long stick to the short stick. The idea is to swing the long stick so that the shorter one slams against the sheaves, knocking the grain from the stem and separating each grain from its husk or chaff.

It's a simple tool, but it takes skill to make the short stick hit along its entire length. Peter needs practice; he either makes only the tip of the short stick strike its target or, worse, he strikes the tip of the long stick he's holding, sending a sudden shock into his hands. With each blow wheat grains sift to the floor. Slowly the threshers circle the heap of wheat sheaves, taking care to hit the stalks and not one another.

After an hour, Father judges that all the grain has been knocked loose. He and the boys gather the stalks, or straw, and put it aside for animal bedding. Now it's time to separate the wheat from the chaff. Luckily there is a gentle breeze blowing just outside the barn door for that step. Father sets a bushel basket just outside the doorway. Then he scoops a smaller basket of grain and chaff from the threshing floor, steps outside and holds it as high as he can while pouring it slowly into the big basket. If the wind is just right, it blows away the chaff while the heavier grain falls into the big basket. A full bushel basket of wheat weighs about 60 pounds.

When all the sheaves have been threshed, Father and the boys pour the grain into hemp sacks and haul them to the front door of the house. All but one or two of the sacks will go up to the attic where it will wait for Mother's baking days. Then they take the rest to the grist mill. There are dozens of mills around the county, but Father likes Herr Stoner's place on Mill Pond just three miles north. It's powered by Tuscarora Creek. Sacks of wheat are hoisted to the top of the mill and poured into chutes that feed the grain to large stone grinding wheels. The wheels pulverize the grains into flour. At the bottom floor of the mill, the flour falls back into sacks. Herr Stoner keeps a little of the flour as his pay.

Father and Stephan take the flour back home. Sometimes Father and the boys take several sacks to Herr Stoner, who buys most of it, and when he has enough, he ships great loads of flour to markets at the coast. In time Herr Stoner's huge Conestoga wagon, pulled by six strong horses, heads east. His mill is on the road to Annapolis and its small seaport. Some Maryland millers take their flour to Baltimore or Philadelphia, where they usually can get a better price for their product. Much of Maryland's flour these days is shipped to the Caribbean to feed slaves working the sugar

cane plantations. Wheat won't grow in the humid tropics, so flour must be imported. In 1769, more than 45,000 tons of flour were shipped out of Baltimore.[21]

WINTER

One morning the family wakes up, and it's surprisingly cold in the house. Mother gets up and stares out the bedroom window at the garden. Delicate traceries of ice festoon the glass. She sees the cucumber vines that trail over the fence have collapsed and turned black. Upstairs the boys pull the feather-stuffed bedding up to their chins and sink down again. They know they're only buying a few minutes.

When the weather turns this cold, it's Stephan's job to get a fire going in the parlor stove. Before Mother can nag him, he stuffs his shirttail (the same shirt serves both day and night) into woolen pants, pulls a coat from a peg and heads down the winding staircase. The necessary fuels were laid in just a week or so before—dried corn husks for tinder, wood shavings from Father's whittling for kindling and a few split oak logs that have been curing for almost a year.

Stephan goes into the kitchen, gets the fire shovel and scoops up some of the last embers of yesterday's cooking fire. The night before, as usual, Mother had banked the fire, heaping ashes over the embers to keep them from dying and setting a copper dome, called a curfew, over it. Kneeling in the center hall, Stephan pushes the embers through an opening in the back of the fireplace and into a big, cast iron box on the other side of the wall. The box is a five-plate stove set against the parlor wall. In go some corn husks and wood shavings. When those are flaming, Stephen lays on two or three sticks of split wood. In a minute he walks into the parlor and touches the stove. As it warms, the iron radiates heat to the parlor and, through a short opening separating the parlor from the small back bedroom, into the space where Father and Mother sleep.

Back in the kitchen, Stephan lays kindling on the remaining embers and lets them catch fire for the breakfast cooking. Mother will keep that same fire going to cook supper. In fact, she keeps at least a few embers going day and night until warm weather returns. That's when cooking switches to the summer kitchen in the attached log house that Grandfather built when he first came to Maryland.

With the cold weather, but before it's freezing during the day, it is time to kill and butcher a hog. Everyone loves pork and sausage and ham and ribs and, especially, bacon. The process takes hours, and the cold air discourages flies and keeps the meat from spoiling before the job is done.

A month or so ago Father had already selected one of his animals to fatten for this year. He brought it up to a small pen near the barn and fed it lots of corn. When the fateful day arrives the whole family pitches in. Stephan makes a fire near the barn to boil water. Mother looks away as Father stuns the animal with a powerful hammer blow to the head, hangs it by its hind legs on iron hooks and slashes open the jugular vein to bleed the animal. Then they pour boiling water over the skin and scrape with knives to remove the bristly hair.

Over the next few hours, the carcass is cut open, cleaned and sliced into various cuts. Each piece is rubbed with handfuls of salt, some of it mixed with pepper. Salt curing will prevent spoilage and draw out moisture, leaving a ham or a rack of ribs good for storing for months. Finally, the pieces of meat are trussed up with hemp twine, taken to the cellar and hung from poles along the ceiling. Eventually some of the pieces of meat will be put in the smokehouse for preservation and flavoring as ham or bacon. Some of the hog will be turned into sausage and scrapple, a traditional German mush made of pork scraps mixed with corn meal, flour and spices. Even the stomach will be cleaned and turned into hog maw, a dish much favored in the old country.

Some of the pork loin is not preserved. It's for supper. Fresh meat is not all that common during most of the year, so this is a special treat. As usual Mother will serve it with sauerkraut, mashed potatoes and apple butter on bread.

Now that most of the labors of early winter are completed—at least those in which the boys must help—it's time for them to go to school. For some years, Herr Schley has been the schoolmaster in Frederick Town. Mother and Father pay him a small sum to instruct the boys in reading, writing and basic arithmetic, which he calls ciphers. The parents have been working with the boys to do this during some evenings at home, but Herr Schley seems to command attention more forcefully. And in the daytime the boys are not tired from a day of work.

Every morning Stephan and Peter walk the mile into town to Herr Schley's log schoolhouse and join several other children for their lessons. The only text for reading is the Bible. There is a small stove in the schoolroom, but still it gets so cold on some days that ink freezes in the pens. The school "year" will continue for nearly three months. When the weather begins to warm the boys will be needed to work on the farm.

One afternoon a few days before Christmas the boys have an earnest discussion about Belsnickel. Peter says he is real. Father and Mother make it seem as if he is real. But Stephen, older and wiser, has figured it out.

Belsnickel is only a frightening character played by a regular person, probably some man in the area. Every Christmas eve he comes to the house, raps on the windows with a long stick, barges in the front door and starts shouting all kinds of strange words. He's dressed in old clothes and ragged furs. His face is blackened. His hair is a fright. Small bells hang from his clothes and jingle as he moves. Peter is not ready to let go of what he has believed for all of his six years.[22]

In the morning of the day before Christmas, Father and Stephan walk out to the woods and saw off an armload of pine boughs. They bring them into the parlor and arrange them on both of the deep window sills. Then they set candles among the boughs and light them. The greenery is a reminder that life continues through the winter and the candle light is a reminder that long, bright days are coming back. Peter lays a pine bough on the warm stove top, and its wonderful scent soon fills the parlor. Everyone keeps an eye on the pine boughs to be sure they don't catch fire.

Mother prepares the feast for Christmas Eve, or *heiliger abend*—holy evening. A ham is roasting on a spit next to the kitchen fire as a kettle of carrots, potatoes and sauerkraut simmers above it. Earlier in the day Mother used some of the dried apple schnitzes to make a pie. There is a fresh loaf of rye bread. From the cellar Father brings up a jug of his best cider.

As this is going on, two of Father's brothers come over with their families. One aunt has brought gingerbread and a brother has a jug of rye whiskey from his still.

Mother and Stephen carry the rest of the meal into the parlor for everyone to enjoy. The boys had set the table with Mother's prized pewter plates as well as knives and forks. Chairs and benches have been brought down from upstairs to accommodate everyone. The hired girl has gone to be with her family in town.

As the meal finishes and the scent of pine fills the room, darkness falls. Suddenly there is a rapping on the parlor window, and a strange man is jumping about outside. Father nods to the window, goes to the front door and begins to open it. Belsnickel bursts inside and jumps into the parlor, bells jingling. The boys are excited, but also scared. The peculiar character asks the boys and their little cousins if they have been good or bad, cracking his whip threateningly. When all the children say they have been good,

Belsnickel throws candy and nuts on the floor. Stephan stoops to pick up the treats, but the frightening ogre cracks his whip at Stephan and demands that he recite a Bible verse. He is finally glad that Mother made him memorize the verse written on the stove in their bedroom from Matthew 6:21: "For where your treasure is, there will your heart be also."

"And where is your treasure?" Belsnickel demands. In heaven, the children reply, whereupon the strange man tosses down a few more goodies and heads out the door, off to visit another family's house.

"I told you he's real," little Peter says to Stephan.

After more talk and more rounds of cider and whiskey, the guests head home, the icy wind feeling a little warmer. Mother says it's time for evening devotions. These religious exercises happen on many evenings through the year, though not as often as Mother would like, especially in summer when there is enough sunlight to work late in the day. There is a prayer, and then Father asks Stephan to read verses from the Bible that tell of Jesus's birth. Fortunately, it's the same book Herr Schley uses in school, so Stephan is familiar with the Fraktur typeface of German Bibles. It's not as easy to read as what the English people use. Peter is asked to read as well. Then the family sings "Es ist ein Ros entsprungen,"[23] (a rose has sprung up) which tells the hopeful story of how in the cold and dark of winter Mary gave birth to a savior. After another prayer, it's off to bed.

But before crawling into the feather bed that the boys share, they stoke fires in all three stoves. This will keep the house well above freezing through the night.

Father knows that the animals should be kept warm as well. Unlike the English farmers who leave their horses, cattle and hogs outdoors through the winter, good German farmers have discovered that in the barn, animals stay warmer and need less hay, corn tops and grain. No fires are needed in the barn; body heat from the animals keeps it comfortable indoors. That's economical, and it provides one other benefit. Because the manure accumulates in a small space, it is easy to shovel up now and then and move to a heap just outside. That happens on winter days when it's unusually nice outdoors, and the animals are let into the barnyard to kick up their heels for a time. When spring comes, Father and Stephan will load the manure onto a low, plank sled, and drag that through the fields, scattering it as they go. Father thinks that a German farmer's fields are greener and more productive than an English farmer's fields, and it is hard to find an Englishman to disagree.

New Year's Day is another time to celebrate. The old year is gone, and it's time to move into the new. As it does every year on this day, the family will be eating pork for good luck because pigs root while moving forward. Chickens and turkeys scratch for their food going backward, which is why they are eaten at the end of the year. It's now time to look ahead. And, of course, to bring a bowl of sauerkraut up from the cellar. Pork-and-sauerkraut is just about as good as a meal can be.

It may be a new year, but there is much work to do before the new growing season can begin. One key task is spinning both flax and wool into thread and yarn. Both fibers have been waiting in baskets in the attic until Mother and the hired girl have time. With the kitchen garden now lying under snow, that time is now. The flax has been retted, broken, scutched, hackled and twisted into small bundles called stricts. Golden filaments almost as long as the girl's arm wait to be spun into thread.

Mother sets up the spinning wheel in the kitchen and adjusts the big drive wheel so that it turns smoothly, its long drive band spinning the small-diameter bobbin many times faster. Mother attaches the distaff, a vertical wooden rod on which she impales several stricts of flax fibers and sits at the wheel. She shows the girl how to pull a few filaments of flax from the distaff and feed them through an orifice and onto the bobbin.

Mother shows the girl how to start by giving a little push to the big wheel and then working the treadle to keep it going. Immediately the bobbin spins, pulling the fibers from her hand and twisting them at the same time. Before the first fibers are pulled entirely onto the bobbin, Mother must overlap their ends to more fibers pulled from the distaff. As she does this, Mother dips her fingers into a cup of water and lays the new fibers alongside the first few. The water activates a natural, sticky substance on the fibers and the spinning keeps them tightly together.

It's a highly skilled process, pulling the right number of new fibers with the left hand and engaging them with the earlier fibers using the right hand and its moisture. At the same time, the feet work the pedals. It's important to keep the number of fibers consistent as the wheel keeps spinning and the thread, now being wound onto the bobbin, grows longer. Mother tells the girl that if the thread, or yarn, varies too much in thickness it won't make smooth linen.

Today the girl watches Mother. Tomorrow she will try her hands at the task. Mother tells the girl that if she spins enough linen thread, she can use it to knit the long stockings that sell well at the market and keep the money.

The homespun linen thread is stored in the attic until there is enough to take to the weaver in town. Weaving requires such complicated equipment and skills that few farmers do it. Of course, there are itinerant weavers who will call at homes, hauling their dismantled looms on wagons. If they find a customer, the weaver reassembles his loom somewhere in the house and goes to work on the thread. Either way, Mother will sew the new fabric into clothing.

Winter is also the best time to fell trees, which Father and Stephan do, mainly to get firewood. Frozen trees are easier to chop and saw then, and if the ground is frozen, it's easier for the horse to drag the logs back to the woodshed. But the main reason is that they are too busy in other seasons. Other than firewood, they need to get the right species of tree to make roofing shingles and split rails to repair the worm fences. Cedar and white oak are good for both because they have straight grain that splits cleanly, and they will resist rot for years.

Still another task this winter is burning limestone to make lime. Every year Father spreads lime on his fields in the spring, along with manure. And he uses the white powder to make plaster to keep the interior walls of the house smooth. If the stones outside the house need new mortar, he can mix lime with sand and water to carry out the repair. And he makes whitewash to keep the insides of the barn and house walls clean and bright. Years ago, he burned chunks of limestone that were lying on the ground or poking up through it. It was those limestone outcrops, along with the big forests, that told Grandfather this was the place to settle. He knew that the soil was fertile and that he could make lime. But Grandfather already collected most of the stone that lay on the surface or was turned up in plowing. Now Father has a little quarry, digging into a hillside where limestone is exposed.

Father and Stephan dig and hammer the rock, breaking off chunks that they carry to the nearby kiln, set in a kind of alcove in the hillside that they quarried two years earlier. First though, they put down a layer of firewood. Then they top it with a layer of limestones, then another layer of firewood. They alternate layers until the pile reaches the top of the hillside, about six feet up.

Making lime is a technology that goes back thousands of years, and to do it right takes skill and experience. The fire must be kept going for ten days and must be tended day and night. Some farmers do it themselves or assign a slave to the task. Father prefers to hire an itinerant lime burner, a man who is willing to camp by the fire every night. The lime burner heaps soil in front of the layers of stone and wood. He pokes holes through the soil for air to enter the furnace. He opens a hole here or closes one there, trying to keep the fire roaring its hottest. The stone must be heated to about 1500 degrees Fahrenheit continuously for ten days. At that temperature, molecules of limestone break down, releasing carbon dioxide which literally wafts out of the stone, turning it into simple lime.

After the requisite time, Father and Stephan head back to the kiln and help the lime burner take down the earthen wall and check on the results. It seems to have gone well. The stones are now white and easily crushed into powder. Come spring most of the lime will be spread on a field and harrowed in. That, plus manure dug from the heap at the barn, will make the fields at Schifferstadt yield abundantly and carry the family through yet another year.[24]

11

Schifferstadt Over the Centuries

Today's stone house has stood more than 260 years, first a mile northwest of Frederick Town but eventually engulfed by the expanding city. Still in its original location, it is on the edge of a leafy residential area and at the western tip of the city's Baker Park, which stretches into downtown. Immediately behind the house is a four-lane federal highway, U.S. 15. The farm that began as 303 acres was sold off in pieces over the centuries, and now slightly more than 1.5 acres remain.

Over the centuries, ownership of the house and land passed through several hands, although it remained in the family until 1899. Brunners and their descendants lived in the house until 1843 when subsequent family owners rented it to tenants, some of whom probably were farming the land. Schifferstadt continued as a rental property and was occupied by tenants until 1973. By that time, after 143 years as a rental, the house had fallen into disrepair, and there was talk of tearing it down to make way for a gas station. In 1974 the newly created Frederick County Landmarks Foundation bought Schifferstadt and began removing attempts at modernization, returning the house close to its condition in the time of the original family.

What follows is a chronology of the chain of ownership and related matters. Some of the details afford a window into the extraordinary disagreements and contentiousness that could arise among Schifferstadt's owners and buyers. Details outlined here, including the spellings of names, are based on official records in government archives. Specifics can be found in the works cited.

1736 – Joseph and Cathrina Brunner and their 13-year-old son, Elias, settle on land in today's Frederick County, Maryland, and build a log cabin. They pay nothing for several years. The land is part of a 7,000-acre tract called Tasker's Chance. Lord Baltimore "patents" the land to Benjamin Tasker, an Annapolis lawyer who becomes the owner.

1744 – Daniel Dulany, another Annapolis lawyer, buys Tasker's Chance, carves it into smaller parcels and lays out city lots for a new Frederick Town.

1746 – Joseph officially buys the 303 acres he has been occupying and farming. He pays Daniel Dulany £10 in the currency of the day, giving him absolute ownership. But he also continues to pay an annual amount, comparable to a property tax, to Dulany. The farm's name enters the record books of Prince George's County, which then included today's Frederick, as Sheverstadt. The deed is dated July 28, 1746 and was recorded on September 20, 1746.[1]

1753 – Joseph sells Sheverstadt and its 303 acres to son Elias for "£200 current money" of Maryland. The deed is dated and recorded on January 17, 1753. The apparent twenty-fold jump in value may reflect several possibilities—rampant inflation, improvements to the property or, most likely, that Joseph had not paid a full purchase price but was enjoying easy terms from the landlord, Daniel Dulany, and making regular rent payments. Joseph's wife, Cathrina, is not mentioned in the paperwork as she surely would have been were she still alive.[2]

1771 – A complicated and frustrating real estate transaction arises. It will drag on for more than 40 years, largely because one buyer will prove to be a difficult and cantankerous man.

On March 21 Elias agrees to sell the house and all 303 acres for £1600 to his brother-in-law Stephen Ramsburgh and, jointly, to Ramsburgh's son-in-law, Christopher Meyer.[3] (Meyer's name is spelled several ways in official records, including Myer, Mayer and Moyer. Here, we stick with Meyer.) Much of the reason for such a huge jump in value is that by this time the large stone house had been built along with other improvements. The farm's name is spelled in official records as Shefferstadt.

On the same day the two potential buyers, Ramsburgh and Meyer, agree informally to divide the property so that Meyer will get the house and 178 acres while Ramsburgh will get the remaining 125 acres which he wants for his son to live on.

But five days later a complication arises. Elias Brunner executes a formal deed and has it recorded with the county conveying the *entire* 303-acre farm to Christopher Meyer for £1,600. Legal ownership of the farm is therefore established in Meyer's name only. But Ramsburgh still wants the 125 acres and makes an agreement in which Meyer says he will convey the 125 acres to Ramsburgh within two months. But that doesn't happen because Meyer and Ramsburgh can't agree where the property line should be drawn. So Ramsburgh engages Charles Beatty to survey the 125 acres as Meyer watches. A fence is built on this line.

But for some reason Meyer still won't give Ramsburgh a deed to the 125 acres.

1779 – Eight years later the dispute is still simmering. Stephen Ramsburg still wants legal possession of the 125 acres that Meyer promised him, but Meyer has not signed the deed, a necessary step. This time Ramsburg doesn't want the land for his son. He wants to sell the 125 acres to Baker Johnson, a lawyer and a brother of Maryland's first governor, Thomas Johnson. Baker Johnson is a partner in ironworks in western Maryland, eventually including the Catoctin Furnace, a smelter and forge ten miles north of Schifferstadt. Some sources suggest that Johnson wanted the land for timber to fuel the furnace.

Even though Ramsburg doesn't hold title to the land, on April 20 he sells it anyway. Baker Johnson buys it for £4,500. This will puzzle later historians since Meyer, not Ramsburg, legally owns all 303 acres that he acquired by deed from Elias Brunner in 1771. But the sale to Johnson is not finalized because Meyer says he needs another survey to determine boundaries of the 125 acres.

1780 – The uncertainty drags on for about a year. This spring another attempt is made to settle the boundary dispute. A new surveyor, Colonel Francis Deakins, with a reputation for accuracy and integrity, surveys the land in the presence of Meyer, Johnson and others. But Meyer still isn't happy. He again refuses to execute a deed for the sale to Johnson. He claims the courses—the direction and distance of each straight line of the survey and the angle to the next point—were reversed in the new survey. This is a known source of error in surveying and can mean that the end-point of a series of metes-and-bounds, as they are called, is nowhere near the beginning point. Meyer says he will hire yet another surveyor at his own expense.

On June 2 Meyer hires Peter Mantz to survey the land. As it turns out, the surveys of Mantz and Deakins match exactly.

So, at last, a deed is drawn up for Meyer and his wife to sign (a wife is routinely required to release her rights of dower). But Meyer then finds a new reason to stall. He claims he needs the rest of the land— the 178 acres he is keeping—surveyed to determine if his remaining acreage is still the same. For months, Meyer delays, claiming that he can't get the surveyor to come.

1782 – Two years later the disagreement boils up yet again. Baker Johnson insists he must have a deed for the 125 acres. The parties arrange for still another survey. Johnson takes Peter Mantz to Meyer's house. He comes up with the same result as the previous two surveyors.

Sensing that progress is at hand, a time is set for Meyer and his wife to sign the deed at last. But instead of bringing his wife to the signing, Meyer claims that Stephen Ramsburgh told him not to execute the deed until all the fencing is removed. Does Ramsburgh think the fencing is his? The outcome is described in court records as "not recorded." There the matter rests a few more years.[4]

1812 – Forty years after the original transaction, Christopher Meyer has finally come to accept the inevitable. Now getting on in years, he writes a will on March 20 bequeathing "all my dwelling plantation ... being part of a tract called Taskers Chance ... containing about one hundred and seventy-eight acres of land." He makes no claim on 125 acres that was disputed for many years.[5]

1815 – Christopher's executor, son John, attests on June 19 that his father had died by this time. John and his brother Israel now jointly own the house and remaining 178 acres.[6]

1821 – The brothers agree on January 20 to divide their father's land. John Meyer receives 27 3/8 acres plus $6,200 from his brother Israel. It appears that there is a house on this land, but not the one known as Sheverstadt, as it is spelled this time. One boundary line of the property is shown beginning at a "stone planted in the main road leading from Frederick Town," today's Rosemont Avenue. Israel receives the balance of the acreage, 151 1/4, and Schifferstadt. The total of the two areas comes to 178 5/8 acres, apparently a more accurate measurement of the property that remained after the 125 acres was carved off.[7]

1824 – John Meyer dies. His will specifies that his sister, Charlotte Birely, is to get his 27 3/8 acres for two years unless she dies first. After that it goes to his brother Israel and their other sister, Ann Mary Doll, now married to Jacob Doll, for five years. The will also lays out some requirements. First Israel is to install 80 segments of post-and-rail fencing "where the rails now lay and should there not be rails enough they are to cut the number which may be deficient." The will even specifies the source of the additional timber—a curiously named parcel "called Puzzlesome Corrected and should there not be post enough in the yard they are to buy the remainder. They are to cut down no wood but to use the fallen and dead timber." [8]

1828 – An important transaction this year is not about Schifferstadt, but does involve parts of other Brunner farms bordering the old homestead. The property in question will be familiar to many 21st century Frederick County residents. In a deed recorded September 2, Elias Brunner, a great-great-grandson of Joseph, the patriarch, sells 88.5 acres plus "10 perches" (a unit of area) to the Justices of the Levy Court in Frederick County for $5,313.75. (A levy court is one that exercises administrative duties much as a county government would.) The deed specifies that the land is to be used in perpetuity "for the Benefit of the Poor of said County and to and for no other use, intent, purpose whatsoever." The Montevue Asylum came to be located on this property. Today the land is occupied by the Frederick County Health Department and the county-owned Citizens Care and Rehabilitation Center & Montevue Assisted Living facility for indigent residents of the county.[9]

1842 – Israel Meyer, owner of Schifferstadt, dies, having willed 101 acres and "30 perches," along with the house, to his son Jonathan. It is identified in the will as "farm or lot #1 recently called Mount Airy." Despite the name change, it is clear that the property includes the Schifferstadt house. It is not clear where the other 50 acres went. Israel's will also mentions a "lot #2," said to be "94 acres, 1 rood and 30 perches." A rood is a quarter acre, and a perch is 1/40th of a rood.[10]

1843 – Jonathan Meyer now sells the 101 acres and 30 perches to Christian Steiner for $3,100.[11] This keeps the farm in the family since Steiner is married to his second cousin Rebecca Weltzheimer, granddaughter of Christopher Meyer, great granddaughter of Stephen Ramsburg and a great-great-granddaughter of Joseph and Catharina Brunner, the original settlers.[12] A month later John Steiner, Israel Meyer's executor, sells a parcel listed as Lot #2, "94 acres 1 rood and 30 perches," to Christian Steiner for $7,130. One boundary line is said to begin in the middle of the road leading from Frederick Town to Brunner's mill.[13] The road will come to be named Rosemont Avenue. The mill, owned by John Brunner (a grandson of Joseph the patriarch), is a fraction of a mile northwest of Schifferstadt.

It appears that Steiner bought the two properties as an investment for he does not live there. From 1843 until the 1970s when the Landmarks Foundation buys it, Schifferstadt is a rental property. As of 1848 Henry Yonson and his family were renting and most likely farming the place. The Yonson family appears on U.S. Census records for 1850, 1860 and 1870 as occupying the Schifferstadt farm. On each of these lists, three generations of the family are shown as members of the household.[14]

1862 – Christian Steiner dies and wills his entire estate, including the house to his son, Dr. Lewis H. Steiner, a physician in Baltimore.[15] For several years the son teaches chemistry and natural history at colleges in the Washington, D.C. area. During the Civil War, Steiner serves as Chief Inspector of the U.S. Sanitary Commission, a private agency authorized by Congress to care for sick and wounded soldiers. After the war he becomes head of the Frederick County School Board and works to improve facilities for African American children.[16]

1892 – Lewis Steiner dies and leaves the property to his wife, Sarah Steiner and their five surviving children, listed in the deed as Bernard C., Gertrude R., Walter R., Bertha R. and Amy L.[17]

1899 – Steiner's heirs sell "Schieverstadt" to Edward C. Krantz for $16,000. Krantz is the first owner not related to the builders and first occupants of the Schifferstadt stone house, Elias and Albertina Brunner. The land now comprises 186 acres 36 perches, "clear of such parts as were heretofore sold off to the City of Frederick."[18]

1926 – Edward C. Krantz dies and leaves the place to his widow, Nannie Krantz. She then conveys title to her sons, Frederick B. Krantz and Henry C. Krantz.[19] In that same year, Henry and his wife Mabel D. Krantz give his brother Frederick B. Krantz two parcels of land from the original homestead. One is listed as about 100 acres; the size of the other is not listed.[20]

1942 – Frederick Krantz dies and leaves everything to his widow, Bessie C. Krantz.[21]

1958 – Bessie C. Krantz and her three daughters transfer almost 18 acres of the remaining land to the Maryland Roads Commission, mainly for the construction of U.S. 15, a highway bypassing downtown Frederick. The amount of compensation is not listed.[22]

1965 – Bessie Krantz, now 77 years old, plans her legacy. She gives a three-quarters interest in the property to her three daughters and keeps a one-quarter for herself.[23]

1969 – Bessie Krantz dies[24] and her daughters—Evelyn A. Krantz, Olive Dinterman and Elizabeth Kirschman—inherit their mother's interest in the property. The three now own all that is left of Schifferstadt. By now almost all of the original land is gone, the house is in serious disrepair and there is talk of using the site, now at an interchange with U.S. 15, for a gas station.

1972 – Four far-sighted Frederick women determine to save Schifferstadt and establish the Frederick County Landmarks Foundation. The four are Ann Lebherz, Margaret "Maggie" Kline, Joan "Birch" Hotz and Fritz "Fritsie" Keller. Two years later, the foundation buys the house and its remaining 1.511 acres for $65,000.[25] The Maryland Historical Trust lends the money. The President of FCLF, Ann Lebherz, receives a brass key to the front door from Evelyn Krantz on July 2, 1974.[26] The foundation hires John Milner of the National Heritage Corporation, a firm that does architectural studies of old buildings. Milner confirms the home's historical value and authenticity.[27] Archaeological digs establish locations of some of the farm's outbuildings and turn up pottery shards and other objects testifying to life at the house in previous centuries.[28] A few of the artifacts are on display in the museum.

1994 – Twenty years after the Landmarks Foundation acquired Schifferstadt, the organization pays off the purchase loan and stages a mortgage burning. *The Frederick News-Post* covers the ritual and writes: "Schifferstadt preserves what may be the most significant example of German Colonial architecture in the United States. The house has been cited in Maryland's top 10 list of historic properties and draws great interest from scholars and descendants of the home's inhabitants. A dedicated group of volunteers keeps the house maintained and open to the public."[29]

12

Schifferstadt Architectural Museum

The house is a large, well-proportioned building made of local sandstone. It typifies German homes that have survived from the American colonial era. Significantly, Schifferstadt exhibits more distinctively German architectural features than any other home in the region. It was those features that led the National Park Service to designate the house a National Historic Landmark, an elite designation reserved for a small percentage of historic properties. The most important of those features are described in this chapter.[1]

And it is the oldest home in Frederick County open to visitors.

In their homeland, Germans built with both stone and wood, often with stone at the ground level and a timber-framed upper story, also called half-timbered or in German, *fachwerk.*[2] Schifferstadt is stone from bottom to top, even though timber was plentiful.

Perhaps the choice of stone represented, even if only subconsciously, a deep commitment to Elias and Albertina Brunners' adopted country. The immigrants had escaped the turmoil and despair of their homeland, endured a difficult and dangerous Atlantic crossing and, likely, years in servitude before they could put down roots and build new lives.

And stone was readily available in the area.

More than that, the choice of stone as a building material suggests that the Brunners, who had the house built in 1758, were well off. Building in stone required the work of a master mason plus apprentices and helpers. Also, the interior demanded skilled carpenters to hew and join the heavy timbers that make up the main inside walls, floor joists and attic framing. Elias may have gained some of the necessary skills, but he certainly needed professional help.

Photo by Boyce Rensberger. Courtesy of the Frederick County Landmarks Foundation

Schifferstadt Architectural Museum. The original house is stone. Brick additions to the left are 19th century constructions on the probable site of the original Brunner log home.

Elias or his master mason, or both, took care to make the front of the house, facing toward Frederick Town, appealing to the eye. This facade is symmetrical, the front door centered between two good-sized windows on the first floor with three on the second floor, all the windows the same dimensions.

The front door opens to a center hall, a design most often associated with the English Georgian style. Although center halls are known in Germany, where such homes are called *durchgängigen haus,*[3] their adoption in America may represent something more. Some architectural scholars have concluded that when German settlers chose the center hall plan, it reflected the owners' wealth and served to distinguish the family from less affluent Germans.

"Significant financial resources were required to build, or even rent, a large, two-story masonry dwelling of the best sort," wrote Cynthia G. Falk, a historian of material culture who studies Pennsylvania Germans. "Such buildings were seen as expressions of social rank ... also that they [the owners] possessed education, social grace, and leadership potential." [4]

Also, they may have wanted to be more like the wealthy and powerful English. We cannot say whether this describes Elias and Albertina, but it seems reasonable that the Brunners' choice of a center-hall house plan indicates that they were on the way up in a multicultural, colonial America.

Most German American homes had no center hall. In many the front door opened to the kitchen, which served as a multipurpose room.[5] In others there were two front doors, one for company that opened to a parlor and another that opened into a kitchen or a workroom for people gathering for a project such as a "schnitzing frolic." [6] Schifferstadt's plan uses the center hall to reach the parlor to the left or the kitchen to the right. The separation of activities into two rooms—parlor and kitchen—is another mark of rising socio-economic status.

The way the stones were laid in the front also speaks of a desire to impress. They are about the same thickness and laid in level courses. Over the door and the two first floor windows are stone "relieving" arches, an ancient method of transferring the weight from above to support on each side of an opening. By contrast, stones in the gable ends of the house and the back are irregular in size and not evenly coursed, a practice called rubble-laid. This avoids the laborious process of shaping the quarried stones into similarly sized blocks.[7] And, of course, it saved money. Elias was well off but frugal.

The stone itself is of local origin, although the quarry site has not been identified. It is one of the many colors of sandstone, light tan-gray in this case. More colorful versions of sandstone were used to make New York City's famous "brownstone" buildings and the Smithsonian "castle" building. Sand for Schifferstadt's mortar probably came from Carroll Creek, which runs through the property, and its lime from any of the local limestone quarries, perhaps one already on the farm.

The facade, not counting the newer attached brick structure (which is discussed below), measures 40 feet 2 ½ inches wide. The house is 30 feet 2 inches deep. The walls of the first story are about two feet thick. Rather than build such a wall with stones large enough (and therefore quite heavy) to make such a thick wall, the traditional practice was to build two walls, one just inside the other with a narrow space between them. The flattest sides of the stones are positioned to face to the outdoors. The next flattest sides are used for the inside wall, facing the interior of the house. Inside stones were plastered over and whitewashed to make a finished surface.[8]

A typical work crew probably followed the ancient practice of one or two master masons plus apprentices and helpers.[9] In this case, the crew might include six men, apprentices on the ground mixing mortar and carrying buckets of it up to master masons at one or more levels of scaffolding, others handing up stones that had been shaped with chisel and hammer, or dressed. Once the twin walls are mortared up a few feet, smaller stones and chips from dressing large stones are poured between the walls, filling the gap. Mortar or perhaps just mud may have been poured into the gap as well.[10]

At intervals the masons did use larger stones that spanned the two walls to become part of each, tying them together for structural stability. As the wall rose, the workmen built higher scaffolding. Horizontal members of the scaffold rested inside small gaps left in the outer wall. Eventually, the gaps were filled with stone as the scaffolding was dismantled.[11] At Schifferstadt's second floor, the walls taper from the inside to about 18 inches in thickness. That's because these walls have less load to bear.

The massive weight of all this stone is borne by the bedrock on which Schifferstadt is built.[12]

On the north gable end, the stonework rises to meet the roofline. The south gable, by contrast, presents a puzzle. Sources differ on what kind of wall met the roof. An insurance policy on Schifferstadt issued in 1848 says this gable end of the main house was frame, i.e., wood.[13] A study done in 1974 considers it likely that a stone wall originally rose to the roofline as it does on the north end but was changed to brick, probably around 1867 when the brick additions seen today replaced the original log structure. It seems that the upper part of the south end of the house may have gone from stone to frame to brick.[14]

The back, or west, wall of the house also has a circuitous history. As viewed from behind the house, there is a door at the end of the center hall and a window on each side. One window opens to the kitchen and the other to a bedroom behind the parlor. The 1974 study notes that the door opening looks to have been cut into the stone wall, as if there had been no door there originally.[15] The window to the right also appears to have been cut into the wall. Both changes may have been part of the 1867 construction that included the brick addition.

When the new openings were made, both the door and the window were left with no relieving arches, making them different from all the other first story openings in the stone walls. The arches that can be seen today were added by the Landmarks Foundation in the 1980s.[16]

The front door, a modern replacement, follows the typical German pattern of having a decorative front surface, in this case a frame-and-panel motif, nailed to a simpler internal door of wide, vertical planks beaded along the edges.[17] The two layers gave extra protection against intruders, perhaps a consideration as the house was built during the French and Indian War when hostilities came close to Frederick.

The current roof sheathing is split cedar shingles, but the original was probably white oak.[18] The topmost course of shingles on the back side extends well above the ridge where it meets shingles on the front. This was a common technique to prevent rain from entering a gap along the ridge.

Prevailing wind being from the west, it cannot blow water into the attic. The rare easterly winds are another story.[19]

One distinctive feature of colonial German rooflines was a so-called kick or flare along the eaves. This is best seen from either gable end of the house. The roof slopes steeply down from the ridge until it suddenly breaks, rising a bit like a ski jump. This effect, apparently purely esthetic, is achieved by using false rafters—wood wedges nailed on top of the main, or common,

The house minus the 1877 additions, viewed from the back. Sketch omits two of the 5-plate stoves (the one that survives is shown) and ignores original log cabin footprint, which was on the right-hand end. *Courtesy of the Frederick County Landmarks Foundation.*

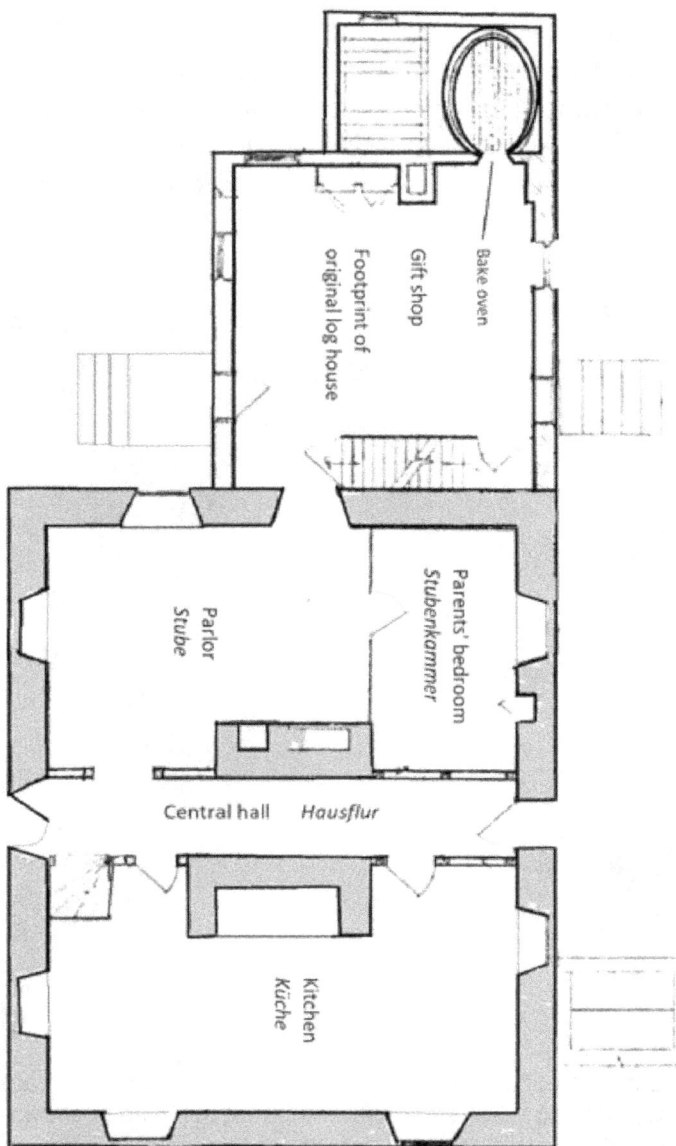

Plan view of the house, original stone walls shaded. Drawing adapted from Restoration Study by John D. Milner et al, 1974. Courtesy of Frederick County Landmarks Foundation.

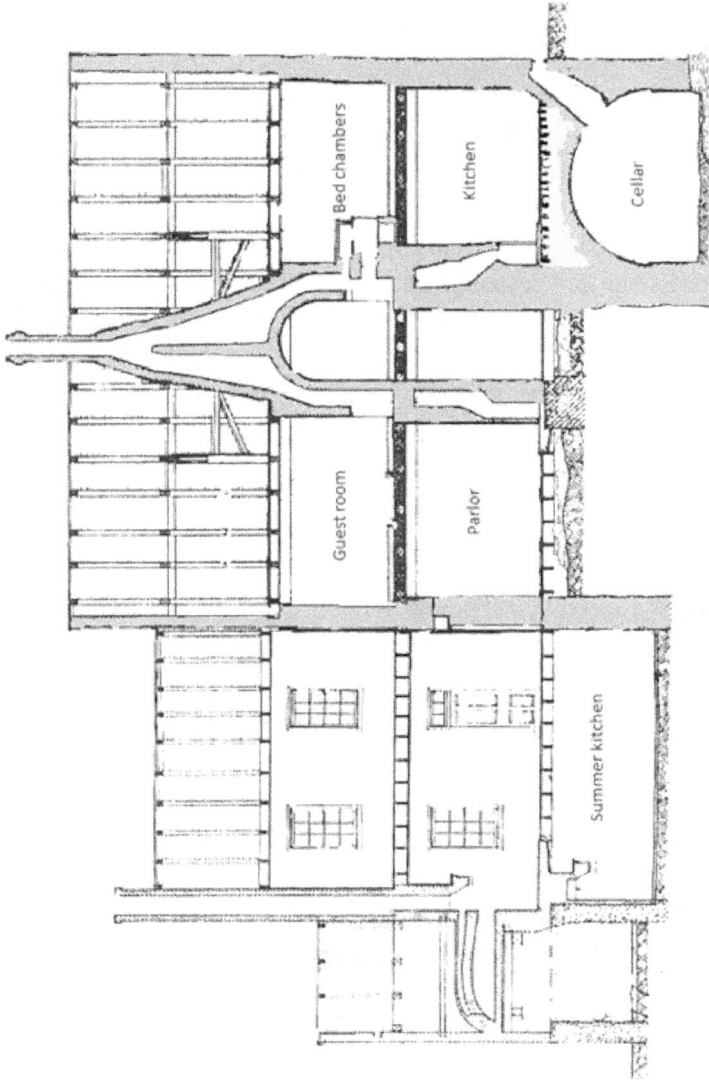

The house in cross section, stone walls shaded. *Adapted from* Restoration Study *by John D. Milner et al, 1974. Courtesy of Frederick County Landmarks Foundation.*

rafters.[20] The rafters were rebuilt in the early 20th century and the kick was made less pronounced than was typical. The roof's steep pitch maximized interior headroom, necessary because this space was a working part of a German farm house. This is discussed below in a section called "The Attic."

Because people lived in the house into the 1970s, the building was modified and updated several times, including by the addition of a bathroom upstairs, which has since been removed.[21] Still, given the centuries the house has existed, relatively few changes were made, and most of the original structure remains intact. One reason is that it was a rental property for about 130 years before the Frederick County Landmarks Foundation acquired it. The Foundation has since removed most of the modifications. The primary goal now is preservation, a costly process.

Inside the Stone House

The Parlor, or *Stube*

Like guests in the days of the Brunners, visitors to Schifferstadt typically begin their tour in the house's parlor or in German, *stube*. It is a sizeable room with a generous nine-foot ceiling, a foot higher than is typical in today's homes.

The parlor is also called a stove room because it originally contained a cast-iron, five-plate stove.[22] This was an exclusively German feature—a clean, energy-efficient, radiant heating system consisting of five cast-iron plates fitted together to make a box. The sixth side was open and fastened against an opening in an interior wall that was accessed from a fireplace in the center hall. Details of this unusual stove design are in the section below called "The North Bedchambers," where one of the originals remains in place. In the *stube*, the stove sat where today there is a small concrete pad that probably supported some other kind of stove installed in later times.

Architectural historian Cynthia Falk has written that the presence of a five-plate stove in a formal front parlor "clearly differentiated the eighteenth-century houses of elite Pennsylvania Germans from those of elite Americans of British descent." [23] No doubt the same was true of Maryland Germans. The Brunners, during their years in Pennsylvania, surely saw how successful Germans designed and outfitted their homes and strived to do the same.

Next to the stove place are built-in cupboards, the doors held by what are called rat-tail hinges.[24] This type of hinge and a variety of other styles around the house suggest the Brunners appreciated artistic expression in the blacksmith's craft.

Photo by Boyce Rensberger. Courtesy of the Frederick County Landmarks Foundation

The parlor, or *stube*, looking toward the partition that separates a small back bedroom. A five-plate stove once sat on the pad at the right.

The cupboard is set into a massive masonry wall that extends up through the second floor to help support the heavy "wishbone" chimney that rises through the center of the roof. Center chimneys are typically German, while the English tended to put chimneys at the gable ends.[25] This massive structure is one of two that support the chimney. The other is in the kitchen where it holds the open-hearth fireplace. (The chimney is discussed further in a section below, "The Upstairs Hall.")

The *stube* was where the family gathered for meals,[26] typically at a long table with benches. In the evenings, the children might practice their letters and numbers at the table, a candle flickering between them. The parlor is where Albertina might sit to do her knitting, Elias to read. On special occasions guests gathered here for meals.

Photo by Boyce Rensberger. Courtesy of the Frederick County Landmarks Foundation
A window in the parlor, showing thick walls and a splayed opening.

During the day, the widely splayed window openings admit more sunlight than would parallel-sided openings in a two-foot-thick wall. The six-over-six sashes are reproductions of a style that was typical for the period and likely existed in the house's early days.[27] Glass was relatively costly, but Frederick did have a glass factory at this time just four miles north of the house,[28] and the Brunners could afford it.

A thin partition at the back of the room separates the parlor from a small bedroom discussed in the next section.

Along the ceiling is one end of a massive oak beam that runs the 40-foot width of the house. In this room it is boxed in. Measuring 8 inches by 10 inches, it is called a summer beam, from an archaic French word, *sommier*, meaning beast of burden. There is an identical beam by the partition that separates the back bedroom. These beams carry much of the weight of the second floor.

The Parents' Bedchamber, or *Stubenkammer*

It was the custom for German parents to sleep in a downstairs room to be able to respond quickly to someone at the front door. Theirs was the *Stubenkammer, kammer* being German for chamber.

Separating the bedroom from the parlor is a thin wood partition, its vertical boards edged with a decorative bead. The wall may not originally have had the large door that is in it now. It is certain, however, that the room could be accessed through a door to the center hall. This opening was closed off many years ago and plastered over. Evidence of the doorway can be seen from the center hall where plaster and lath have been removed. The board partition did have the small door that is in it now, just 45 inches tall. This was to allow heat to radiate from the (now absent) stove into the bedroom.[29]

The room is small, barely large enough for a double bed and a chest or two. Its most distinctive feature is a wall safe with a frame-and-panel door attached by highly decorative rams-horn hinges.[30] Their presence here is another indication that the Brunners were sufficiently well off that they did not need to settle for the plainest hardware from the blacksmith. This is where the family kept money and other valuables, which may have included legal papers and the family Bible.

The bedroom is displayed with a reproduction of the type of bed the Brunners surely used—a rope bed and the tool used to tighten ropes that have stretched. Coil spring mattresses would not be invented for another century or so. Over the ropes is a featherbed, essentially a comforter stuffed with feathers.[31] In winter Germans traditionally used a second featherbed over themselves.

Photo by Boyce Rensberger. Courtesy of the Frederick County Landmarks Foundation

A bed inside the back bedroom, or *stubenkammer*, where Elias and Albertina slept.

Photo by Boyce Rensberger. Courtesy of the Frederick County Landmarks Foundation

A "wall safe" set into the back wall of the bedchamber, notable for the fancy ram's-horn hinges.

The Center Hall, or *Hausflur*

This passageway, as displayed in the architectural museum, affords a look at some of the construction methods used to build the house and, later, to update it. On the south side (left side as if coming in the front door) a section of plaster has been removed to reveal the arched opening originally used to feed a five-plate stove in the parlor. That same wall has been opened to show the original doorway to the little back bedroom. It was closed up and covered with lath and plaster on both sides of the wall, probably as part of a major updating of the house in 1866 or 1867.

The hall walls, both here and on the floor above, were made two different ways. The center parts of each wall, as mentioned above, are thick, load-bearing masonry (stone, brick and mortar) that support a massive chimney in the attic. Flanking the masonry, the hall walls are half-timbered, or *fachwerk*. This method of construction uses wooden posts set vertically for support, often with beams at angles for bracing. Between the posts the wall is filled in with brickwork called nogging.[32] This is exposed in a small section of the wall next to the front door into the kitchen. When the house was new, the bricks were plastered smooth and whitewashed to provide a clean, bright surface. The wood lath and plaster that have been exposed on parts of the walls and ceiling were later modifications.

Posts in the south wall of the hall have grooves indicating that they once held wooden paling—horizontal wood slats (roughly one by three inches) set at intervals to support an infilling of straw and mud, laced into position with twine. When dry the whole arrangement was plastered smooth and flush with the timbers, then whitewashed.[33] While the upstairs hall retains this method of construction, on the first floor some of the paling has been replaced by brick nogging.

The two summer beams, here exposed, can be seen in the hall as they stretch from one end of the house to the other. They and the ceiling bear marks of later lath and plaster that have been removed to reveal the original materials. Analysis indicates that these beams were originally exposed and whitewashed.[34] The summer beams are chamfered, the corners having been planed to a 45-degree angle. This probably was done to make the beams look more finished, but some have suggested that chamfering eliminates the sharp 90-degree angle that left a thinner edge of wood that could catch fire more easily.

The hall ceiling joists—beams that run at right angles to the summer beams—rest on top of the summer beams, in contrast to the English method of dovetailing joists into the summer beam.[35] The English method of joinery can be seen today in several basements around Frederick. The joists are bridged by paling. Wrapped around and stuffed between the slats, as in the walls, was a mixture of mud and straw. When dry the surfaces were plastered smooth and whitewashed.

Photo by Boyce Rensberger. Courtesy of the Frederick County Landmarks Foundation

The downstairs center hall, or *hausflur*. The parlor is through the door at the left. On the hall wall, plaster has been removed to show where the fireplace opening was to feed a five-plate stove in the parlor.

The Kitchen, or *Küche*

The heart of an 18th century German home, as it has become for many in today's America, was the kitchen. The huge, open-hearth fireplace usually had a fire going at all times except during the hottest months, when cooking moved to the summer kitchen in the ground floor, on the probable footprint of the Brunners' original log house. It lies below today's gift shop.

Photo by Boyce Rensberger. Courtesy of the Frederick County Landmarks Foundation

The open hearth fireplace in the kitchen.

In the main kitchen, the fire usually was in one corner of the space, the rest occupied by various pots and kettles some hanging from hooks suspended from an iron bar that spanned the upper part of the opening. Sometimes a second fire was made or some of the coals raked to the other side and a baking or roasting pan, sometimes called a Dutch oven, set on top.

Photo by Boyce Rensberger. Courtesy of the Frederick County Landmarks Foundation

The kitchen, fireplace at the right.

At some point, the space now shown as the kitchen was two rooms, a big one with the fireplace and a smaller one occupying the front third of the space. The now vanished board partition has left its imprint on the plaster and paint that remain on the wall. The smaller room may have served as a pantry and perhaps as an auxiliary bedroom. It may have been here that the spinster worked her skills and, at another time, where an itinerant weaver set up his loom. And, being near the warmth of a kitchen fire, it may sometimes have been what the English called a borning room—a place for women to give birth and and to spend their first days with the baby.

A distinctive German feature of the kitchen is the sink, a shaped piece of stone set under a window sill. Its shallow bowl is inside the room and its spout outside. When wastewater was poured into the bowl, it flowed

Photo by Boyce Rensberger. Courtesy of the Frederick County Landmarks Foundation

The kitchen sink, which lets water flow under the window and spill through a spout outside.

under the window, probably into a bucket or barrel set outside under the spout. The water may have been used in the kitchen garden.

Next to the rear door from the hall into the kitchen is a second door. At first glance it seems like a redundant opening to the kitchen. Originally it was the opening to a ladder or steep staircase that led down to the cellar directly under the kitchen. The steps were closed off from the kitchen by a wooden housing.[36] To get something to cook, it was necessary to go out into the hall, open the adjacent door and climb downstairs. The enclosure was removed long ago. The door itself bears yet another hinge design, this one resembling a three-leaf clover.

Where the north wall meets the floor visitors sometimes notice two curious mounds, each about the size of a child's backpack. Inside each of these is an air shaft that connects the cellar to the air outdoors. The external openings can be seen by standing outside the north end of the house. Decoratively shaped wrought iron bars keep larger animals out. The air shafts can be seen from inside the cellar and are discussed below in the "Cellar" section.

The Staircase

It is a tight helix, climbing to the second floor on wedge-shaped treads called winders that can be a bit precarious to use. Still, German builders often preferred this form, commonly known today as a spiral staircase. Though more difficult to build than a stairway of straight flights, it saves usable floor space, a factor that pragmatic Germans surely appreciated.

The staircase now in Schifferstadt is thought to have been rebuilt at some point before 1790 in the same location.[37] Centuries later it remains remarkably stable and creak-free.

The Upstairs Hall

The most striking feature of this hall is the large, white, masonry arch in the middle. This is the most visible part of the house's so-called wishbone chimney.[38] Flues from the kitchen fireplace and the now-absent stove in the parlor rise within the thick part of the walls on each side of the hall and then curve from each side to meet in the arch. There they join two more flues, one from a stove on each side of the upstairs hall. Smoke and hot gases from all four flues merge in a single chimney that rises directly above the arch. In the attic is the massive brick chimney that channels smoke and gases through the roof. The arch is needed to support the great weight of the chimney, transferring the load to the masonry supports

Photo by Boyce Rensberger. Courtesy of the Frederick County Landmarks Foundation

The upstairs center hall with an arch that carries the load of a massive center chimney directly above. Fireplace opening at the left feeds the five-plate stove in the bedrooms. Steps at the far end lead to the attic.

on each side. The arch has the secondary benefit of increasing the surface area within the living space that is warmed by heat rising from the fires.

English houses often put fireplaces and chimneys at the gable ends, especially in Mid-Atlantic and southern colonies. The wishbone chimney is a creative solution to the German tradition of a central chimney but here it is set squarely above the center hall that the more affluent English liked. It is a hybrid arrangement, but to be sure, it is known from other German houses in the old country.

The south hall wall is of *fachwerk* construction that originally was not plastered over. "This is a significant architectural feature as it is the first example of exposed wall framing of this type to be recorded in Maryland," according to an architectural historian who examined the building for the Maryland Historical Trust.[39]

The North Bedchambers, or *Kammern*

On the north side of the upstairs hall are two similar bedrooms separated by a partition one board thick. The boards are impressively wide, and hand-planing is obvious with the raking illumination of a spotlight.[40] The highlight of these rooms, however, is the black, cast-iron, five-plate stove mounted at the hall end of the partition so that it can heat both rooms. These are also called jamb stoves.

Perhaps more than any other feature of Schifferstadt, this stove speaks of the German heritage of the house and, for that matter, of Frederick County. It was prominent among the many German characteristics that merited designation of the house as a National Historic Landmark. Although such stoves were common to the more affluent early German homes in America, this is the only one known to remain in its original location.[41] A few are in museums.

Its three, cast-iron side plates are decorated with traditional German motifs including geometric patterns, tulips and stars under arches supported by twisting columns. The plain top and bottom plates are edged with channels to hold the side plates. Tabs at the ends of the top and bottom plates have holes for a long, vertical bolt that clamped all the plates tightly together. The bolt is missing in this case. Vertical iron channels secure the two outside corners.

Unlike a modern wood stove, it does not have an obvious fuel door. Instead the sixth side is open and fastened against a chimney within the thick masonry wall separating the twin bedrooms from the hall. The hall side has an opening that looks like a small fireplace through which the stove was fed. A fire is built in the stove; its smoke vents through a duct in

Photo by Boyce Rensberger. Courtesy of the Frederick County Landmarks Foundation
The most distinctively German feature of the house is this five-plate stove.
It is the only one in America known to be in its original location.

the top of the firebox and into the flue, and the iron plates heat up. Having no legs, the stove rests on non-combustible masonry.

Clean, radiant heat filled the rooms with warmth but not smoke or ash; sparks were safely contained within the stove. And there is none of the draft of open, English-style fireplaces that must pull in outside air to replace what is sent up the chimney. In this case the draft flows through the hall, not the rooms being heated.[42] This kind of stove also was energy efficient. In fact, it used only a quarter to a fifth as much wood to heat a room as did an open fireplace, according to no less a figure than Benjamin Rush, a leader of early American science and medicine and a signer of the Declaration of Independence.[43]

Photo by Boyce Rensberger. Courtesy of the Frederick County Landmarks Foundation
One side of the five-plate stove, carrying the last part of a Bible verse and, at the bottom, the date of 1758. The top part of the 8 is incomplete.

Wrapped around the stove's three vertical sides is a verse from the Bible in all caps: "*Wo euer Schatz ist da ist auch euer Herz.*" It's from Matthew 6:21 and Luke 12:34. In English it says, "For where your treasure is, there also is your heart." The meaning becomes clearer from the Biblical context that advises believers to store their treasure in heaven. Molded into the end plate are the names Jahn B. and H. Stig, now somewhat damaged, which stand for Jahn Barr and Henry Stiegel. Barr and Stiegel owned the Elizabeth Furnace, an iron foundry near Lititz in Lancaster County, Pennsylvania that specialized in making five-plate stoves.[44]

Most crucially for historical purposes, the two side plates bear the date of 1758. The 8 is incomplete, probably as a result of having been cast in a damaged mold. The flaw led some earlier observers to misread the date as 1756. The date is the strongest clue as to when the house was built. This is because five-plate stoves are not easy to add to an existing house. They require fireplace-shaped openings to be built in the adjoining wall (in the center hall in this case). And they need fireproof masonry bases plus accommodations for an exhaust flue to enter the chimney. All these are most easily done while the house is under construction. The 1974 "Restoration Study," commissioned by the Frederick County Landmarks Foundation, concluded that "the house was designed to contain three five-plate stoves." [45]

When Elias was building the house, he knew that he wanted to heat his home with such stoves and ordered them from the foundry in Lancaster County in 1758 or soon after. A mystery is why he accepted plates with imperfect casting. Perhaps frugality came into play again.

The Guest Room, or *Kammer*

This is the largest bedroom in the house. It could have been made available to special guests such as itinerant judges or clergymen or perhaps a tutor hired for the children. Public accommodations in Frederick Town in those days, typically taverns or inns, usually offered minimal comforts. Well-to-do families such as the Brunners often took pride in hosting important visitors. And since travel was more arduous in those days, guests might stay for days or weeks and would be put up in the best room in the house. Hospitality to travelers once was a characteristic of many traditional cultures.[46]

This room originally had a five-plate stove like the one across the hall. Plaster has been removed from the hall wall to show the original fireplace opening. At some point the stove was removed and the heating system converted to a conventional, if wasteful, open, English-style fireplace.

The one-board-thick partition at the back of this room walled off a space that may have been another small bedroom. When the house was occupied in modern times, it was a bathroom. Today, its fixtures removed, it is used as a storage space.

The Summer Kitchen, or *Sommerküche*

One way of beating the heat in summer was to move cooking operations away from the main house and into a smaller kitchen outside the stone walls. Many colonial homes had a separate building for cooking in summer, but the Brunners appear to have used a space already attached to their house. It was inside a log building that stood on this spot. That structure was torn down around 1867 and replaced with the two-story brick building that today holds the gift shop and Landmarks Foundation office. The summer kitchen lies directly under the gift shop.

Most of the bricks in the floor are badly worn and broken and may have been part of the earlier log house, which, according to an 1848 insurance policy, stood a story and a half tall.[47]

Eighteenth century carpenters' tools of the kind used to build the wooden parts of the house are on display in this room. They range from a felling axe to planes for putting decorative edges on boards such as the beads in board partitions around the house.

The Cellar, or *Kellar*

Visitors are often struck by how the temperature drops as they walk from the summer kitchen through a narrow passageway to the cellar. This is because while the south end of the summer kitchen is only slightly below ground level, the house is set into a slope that rises to the north. Thus, the level passageway from the kitchen to the cellar effectively tunnels into a cave. The earthen cellar floor is about 10 feet below ground level. The passageway was not original to the house but probably was excavated when the footprint of the original log cabin was enlarged for the 1867

Photo by Boyce Rensberger. Courtesy of the Frederick County Landmarks Foundation

The summer kitchen, possibly on the footprint of the original log house.

brick building. That's when the limestone wall of the passageway was laid to serve as a foundation for the back wall of the main house.

Lying directly beneath the main kitchen, the cellar was the refrigerator of the 18th century. Baskets of apples and crocks of sauerkraut stood on the floor. Various fruits and vegetables were stored on shelves along the sides. Smoked or salted meats hung from poles along the barrel-vaulted ceiling, a design typical in German homes in both the old country and the new.

Photo by Boyce Rensberger. Courtesy of the Frederick County Landmarks Foundation

Directly under the kitchen, this barrel-vaulted cellar was the refrigerator of the 18th century. With the floor ten feet below grade, it is nearly as cool as a cave. In winter, colder outside air flows in through two air shafts, one obvious at the left.

High on the north side are two air shafts that connect the cellar to outside air. These allow warmer air to escape and cold winter air to flow into the cellar, dropping its temperature still further during the months when fresh produce was not available, and fall's bounty needed to be kept as cold as possible.

The wall at the far end contains an arched niche, looking as if it should hold a saint's statue. Its function is unclear, but it is frequent feature in old, German cellars. Perhaps it was a more rodent-resistant spot for cheese. Milk and butter might also have been kept here.

At the opposite end of the cellar are masonry steps that climb up to bulkhead doors at ground level. These provided easy access from the kitchen garden behind the house. Access from inside the house was through a door at the back end of the center hall. It led to steps or perhaps only a ladder that descended into the cellar. This was removed, probably when the passageway was opened from the summer kitchen.

The Attic

Schifferstadt's attic is a large space, quite unlike the cramped versions in modern homes. At the center, the ceiling is 13 feet, 4 inches high. The space was used for storage and, no doubt, as sleeping accommodations if there were too many in the house for its four bedrooms. Honored guests, of course, would have had the large guest room, but their children and servants could find plenty of room up top.

The windows in each gable end, one with a southern exposure, provide a fair amount of daylight for routine tasks.

As with other homes of German immigrants, the attic was where the family stored its grain and other foodstuffs such as dried beans and peas that didn't need the cold temperature of the cellar. It must have been awkward hauling sacks or baskets of grain up the winding stairs, but it is well documented that this was a common procedure.[48] In fact, the practice continued in Germany into the 20th century. After all, with a good roof, the attic was dry and safe from thieves, at least of the larger sort that might raid a barn. No doubt mice were a problem everywhere. Culinary and medicinal herbs were hung from the attic beams to dry.

According to one source, the custom in Europe was to keep all the farm's grain in the attic and to take only one bag at a time to the miller to be ground into flour.[49]

Two features of Schifferstadt's attic are most striking. One is the massive brick chimney stack in the middle of the space, shaped like a steep pyramid. Here is where flues from stoves and fireplace join and rise through the roof. Its great weight is obvious and explains the thick parts of the interior walls of the house's first and second floors, load-bearing walls indeed.

Photo by Boyce Rensberger. Courtesy of the Frederick County Landmarks Foundation

In the attic, a massive pyramid of bricks contains flues
from four fireplaces.

The other feature is the timber framing that supports the roof. To the untrained eye, beams seem to stretch every which way. But there is a careful geometry to it, especially the part nearest to the chimney. It is built according to a German system called *Liegender Stuhl*, which literally means "reclining chair." [50] Unlike a chair with vertical legs, this system has beams, or struts, set at slanting angles. Because it does

Photo by Boyce Rensberger. Courtesy of the Frederick County Landmarks Foundation

Huge wood beams in the attic follow a complicated but traditional German design for supporting a roof while leaving the floorspace uninterrupted.

not need vertical posts, this design leaves the attic floor space uninterrupted and thus more practical for work and storage. It also reduces the sideways force that a heavy roof can exert on exterior walls. The system was common in Central Europe beginning in the 15th century, and German carpenters brought it to America.

Elsewhere on the Farm

The stone house is all that remains of the early farmstead. But some idea of Schifferstadt in its heyday comes from an 1848 insurance policy describing other structures in use at that time.

Some 250 feet east of the house there was a large, stone barn measuring about 58 feet by 40 feet—about twice the size of the main house. Nearer the house, just 85 feet east, stood a large frame building described as a "wagon shed and corn cribs," measuring 29 feet by 31 feet. The farmstead also included a log-built sheep shed measuring about 20 feet by 15 feet and a smokehouse measuring 13 feet square. The policy also records various other smaller farm buildings.[51] Many of these stood where today there is a church parking lot, across Second Street.

Archaeological investigations have found that there was a circular well 20 feet from the southwest corner of the house. Measuring six feet in diameter, it had an 18-inch thick limestone wall. Farther away from the house there once stood a privy, its pit found to contain pieces of broken ceramics and other discarded artifacts.[52]

In the 20th century, a wooden barn of a type called Sweitzer or Swisser (likely for its origin in Switzerland), stood where the church parking lot is today. Another insurance policy, from 1867, notes the existence of a "new barn" in that location. Although there is a 1963 photograph of what likely was that same barn, it and all the other outbuildings of Schifferstadt have long since vanished without a trace. Or, at least, they vanished without a trace that can be seen today. Quite likely traces remain under the parking lot pavement, accessible only to archaeologists of the future.

Today's Gift Shop

This room and the one directly above, which houses the Landmarks Foundation office, are entirely different from what existed in the Brunners'

Schifferstadt's barn is visible here in the background of this 1963 photograph shot from behind the house. It may be one that was built in the 1860s. It has long since been torn down. *Courtesy Carl Brown Collection (MR4), Maryland Room, C. Burr Artz Public Library, Frederick County Public Libraries.*

time, even within their log house. The only part usually described on tours is the squirrel-tail oven in today's gift shop, which may have been built during the 19th century reconstruction of this part of the house. Or it may be older. The 1848 insurance policy describes a bake oven attached to the log building.

It is a large oven, a longish dome of bricks over a brick floor that could hold dozens of loaves. To use it, a fire was built inside and fed until the bricks became as hot as needed. A distinctive feature of the oven is an internal flue set in a channel that begins at the back of the oven and arches over the dome toward the front. Its shape gave rise to the name of this as a squirrel-tail oven. (Imagine the shape of a squirrel's tail curved over the animal's back and then curling up at the tip.) The flue at the back draws heat from a fire near the front, spreading it the length of the oven. With heat from both sides, the bricks heat up very quickly. Then the coals were raked out and the dough put in with the use of a peel much like pizza bakers use today. The opening was blocked with a cast iron plate.[53]

After baking, residual heat in the oven could be used to dry corn, beans or peas.[54]

* * * * *

The home of Elias and Albertina Brunner has stood for more than 260 years, a testament to the durability of 18th century German methods of designing and building a house. Also, it is evidence that the promise made by the colonial proprietors of Pennsylvania and Maryland was good. America really was a land of opportunity where immigrants desperate to escape bad situations could make new and better lives. The house that stands today welcomes visitors who want to know more about a way of life that built America.

NOTES

Abbreviations of Sources

AOMOL   Archives of Maryland Online

FCCLR   Frederick County Court (Land Records)

FCG   Frederick County Government

MSA   Maryland State Archives

PGCCLR   Prince George's County Court (Land Records)

ROWFCM   Register of Wills, Frederick County, Maryland

All web addresses (URLs) have been verified as of February 12, 2019.

Chapter 1. A Horrific Homeland

1. Donald Lewis Osborn, *Joseph Brunner of Rothenstein, Schifferstadt, and Frederick* (Lee's Summit: Donald Lewis Osborn, 1991), 11-30.

2. William Beidelman, *The Story of the Pennsylvania Germans, Embracing an Account of Their Origin, Their History, and Their Dialect* (Easton: Express Book Print, 1898), 18, https://archive.org/details/cu31924028864259/page/n7.

3. Peter H. Wilson, *Europe's Tragedy: A New History of the Thirty*

Years War (London: Penguin, 2010), 787.

4. David Herlihy, et. al., "History of Europe, Demographics," *Encyclopædia Britannica*, https://www.britannica.com/topic/history-of-Europe/Demographics.

5. Beidelman, *The Story of the Pennsylvania Germans*, 21.

6. Osborn, *Joseph Brunner of Rothenstein*, 11.

7. Beidelman, 27-28.

8. Grace L. Tracey and John P. Dern, *Pioneers of Old Monocacy: The Early Settlement of Frederick County, Maryland, 1721-1743* (Baltimore: Genealogical Publishing Co., Inc., 1987), 269. The authors note that Klein Schifferstadt was known as "upper village" while Gros Schifferstadt was known as "lower village."

9. Frank Ried Diffenderfer, *The German Exodus to England in 1709. (Massenauswanderung Der Pfälzer)* (Lancaster: n.p., at the request of the Pennsylvania-German Society, 1897), 262-265. https://archive.org/stream/germanexodustoen07diff#page/n4/mode/1up.

10. Marion Dexter Learned, Ph.D., L.H.D., *The Life of Francis Daniel Pastorius, The Founder of Germantown* (Philadelphia: William J. Campbell, 1908), 220, 223, https://archive.org/stream/lifefrancisdani00leargoog#page/n8/mode/1up.

11. Osborn, 17.

12. Arta F. Johnson, *Kinfolk in Germany, Kinfolk in Maryland, the Klein Schifferstadt origins & relationships of the families who settled in Maryland: Brunner, Gotzendanner, Sturm, Thomas* (Columbus: A.F. Johnson,1983), 26-27. On Johann Jacob Brunner's church marriage record, his father Joseph's occupation is shown as "des Gerichts" meaning "of the court."

13. Walter Allen Knittle, *Early Eighteenth Century Palatine Emigration; a British Government Redemptioner Project to Manufacture Naval Stores* (Philadelphia: Dorrance & Company, 1937), 4-5, https://archive.org/stream/earlyeighteenthc00knit#page/n7.

14. Juan José Sánchez Arreseigor, "Winter Is Coming: The Deep Freeze of 1709," *National Geographic History*, February 2017, 18-

21, https://www.nationalgeographic.com/archaeology-and-history/magazine/2017/01-02/1709-deep-freeze-europe-winter/.

15. George Fleming, F.R.G.S., *Animal Plagues: Their History, Nature, and Prevention* (London: Chapman and Hall, 1871), 238-239, https://archive.org/details/animalplaguesthe00flem.

16. George Barger, *Ergot and Ergotism/ : A Monograph Based on the Dohme Lectures Delivered in Johns Hopkins University, Baltimore* (London: Gurney and Jackson, 1931), 71, https://archive.org/stream/b29826615#page/n5.

17. Knittle, *Early Eighteenth Century Palatine Emigration*, 5.

Chapter 2. A New Frontier Beckons

1. Daniel Wunderlich Nead, *The Pennsylvania-German in the Settlement of Maryland* (Lancaster: Press of the New Era Printing Company, 1914), 5-11, https://archive.org/details/pennsylvaniagerm22nead.

2. Frank Ried Diffenderfer, *The German Immigration into Pennsylvania through the Port of Philadelphia from 1700 to 1775: Part II: The Redemptioners* (Lancaster: F.R. Diffenderfer, 1900), 97, https://archive.org/details/germanimmigratio00diffuoft.

3. Beidelman, 41.

4. Albert Bernhardt Faust, *The German Element in the United States* (Boston and New York: Houghton Mifflin Company, 1909), 61-63, https://archive.org/stream/germanelementin07fausgoog#page/n12.

5. Gottlieb Mittelberger, *Gottlieb Mittelberger's Journey to Pennsylvania in the Year 1750 and Return to Germany in the Year 1754: Containing Not Only a Description of the Country According to Its Present Condition, but Also a Detailed Account of the Sad and Unfortunate Circumstances of Most of the Germans That Have Emigrated, or Are Emigrating to That Country*, trans. Carl Theodor Eben (Philadelphia: J.J. McVey, 1898), 38, https://archive.org/details/gottliebmittelbe00gott.

6. Ralph Beaver Strassburger, *Pennsylvania German Pioneers; a Publication of the Original Lists of Arrivals in the Port of Philadelphia*

from 1727 to 1808, ed. William John Hinke, vol. 1 of 3 (Norristown: Pennsylvania German Society, 1934), 18, https://archive.org/stream/ pennsylvaniagerm42stra#page/n15. Note: Sturm is spelled "Storm" on this list.

Chapter 3. Not So Fast

1. Osborn, 54. Also: Werner Hacker, "American Emigrants from the Territories of the Bishopric of Speyer," transl. and edit. Don Yoder, *Pennsylvania Folklife Magazine*, Summer 1972, 44, https:// digitalcommons.ursinus.edu/pafolklifemag/49/. Note: It's impossible to calculate an accurate relative value between 18th century currency and that of the United States today. In colonial Maryland much of the economy was based on tobacco, the price of which fluctuated wildly. There was also a constant shortage of coin and currency, making barter a common means of transacting business. If the purpose of equating currency between then and now is to compare lifestyles, again it would be inaccurate because specific financial facts, such as income and the cost of various necessities in the 18th century, is lacking. Currency calculators are available on the internet for interested readers, but they are based on broad estimates of economic conditions in the 18th century.

2. Hacker, "American Emigrants from the Territories…," 44.

3. Gottlieb Mittelberger, *Gottlieb Mittelberger's Journey to Pennsylvania*, 18.

4. Faust, *The German Element in the United States*, 68.

5. Mittelberger, 18.

6. Faust, 61.

7. Beidelman, 44.

8. Karl Frederick Geiser, Ph.D., *Redemptioners and Indentured Servants in the Colony and Commonwealth of Pennsylvania*, Supplement to the *Yale Review*, August 1901 (New Haven: The Tuttle, Morehouse & Taylor Co., 1901), 71. https://archive.org/details/ redemptionersind01geis.

9. Strassburger, *Pennsylvania German Pioneers,* xxxi.

10. Strassburger, xxxiv.

11. Mittelberger, 20.

12. Klaus Wust, *"Feeding the Palatines: Shipboard Diet in the Eighteenth Century,"* 32, https://loyolanotredamelib.org/php/report05/articles/pdfs/Report39Wustp32-42.pdf.

13. Henry Eyster Jacobs, Rev., *The German Emigration to America, 1709-1740* (Lancaster: Press of the New Era Printing Company, 1898), 112-113, https://catalog.hathitrust.org/Record/001670172.

14. Beidelman, 49.

15. Hacker, 43. Henry's name appears as "John Henderick" in this source.

16. Strassburger, 29.

17. Strassburger, xxvi.

18. Beidelman, 45-46.

19. Beidelman, 48.

Chapter 4. Pennsylvania

1. Gary B. Nash and Billy G. Smith, "The Population of Eighteenth-Century Philadelphia," *The Pennsylvania Magazine of History and Biography*, July 1975, 362-368, https://journals.psu.edu/pmhb/article/view/43167/42888.

2. "Benjamin Franklin's German Newspaper *Philadelphische Zeitung*," *The Encyclopedia of Greater Philadelphia*, http://philadelphiaencyclopedia.org/archive/immigration-and-migration-colonial-era/11625-wu999_v1_001/.

3. "From Benjamin Franklin to Peter Collinson, 9 May 1753," *Founders Online*, National Archives, last modified June 13, 2018, http://founders.archives.gov/documents/Franklin/01-04-02-0173. [Original source: The Papers of Benjamin Franklin, vol. 4, July 1, 1750, through June 30, 1753, ed. Leonard W. Labaree. New Haven: Yale University Press, 1961, pp. 477–486.]

4. Benjamin Rush, *An Account of the Manners of the German Inhabitants of Pennsylvania*, intro. and annot. Theodore E. Shmauk

(Lancaster: Pennsylvania German Society, 1910), 52, https://archive.org/details/accountofmanners00rush/page/n8.

5. Beidelman, 161.

6. Lawrence Henry Gipson, *Lewis Evans, to which is added Evans' 'A Brief Account of Pennsylvania', Together with Facsimiles of His Geographical, Historical, Political, Philosophical, and Mechanical Essays, Numbers I and II...Also Facsimilies of Evans Maps* (Harrisburg: Historical Society of Pennsylvania, 1939), as quoted in Richard H. Shryock, "British Versus German Traditions in Colonial Agriculture," *The Mississippi Valley Historical Review*, June 1939, 39–54, https://www.jstor.org/stable/1893205.

7. Dieter Cunz, *The Maryland Germans: A History* (Princeton: Princeton University Press, 1948), 7.

8. Pennsylvania State Archives,"Records of the Land Office, Philadelphia County," Warrant Registers, 1733-1957. Series #17.88, October 26, 1734, Warrant #8, Book A49, page 49. http://www.phmc.state.pa.us/bah/dam/rg/di/r17-88WarrantRegisters/PhiladelphiaPages/r17-88PhiladelphiaPageInterface.htm. Note: The family name is spelled "Gratzendanner" in the index.

9. Harold Smeltzer, *Hanâ Jacob Brunner Family, Duttwiler to Cocalico* (Burnham: Harold Smeltzer, 1994), pp. 3, 6. Land records in Pennsylvania indicate that a warrant for a tract of land in West Cocalico Township, Pennsylvania was received by Jacob Brunner in 1735. This documentation, located at Lancaster History, Lancaster, PA, shows that this landholder was Hanâ Jacob Brunner of Duttweiler, Rhineland-Pfalz, Germany, not Jacob Brunner of Schifferstadt, Rhineland-Pfalz, Germany and Frederick, Maryland.

10. "Historical Treasure-Trove," *The Daily News*, (Frederick, MD), September 4, 1895, 3, microfilm at the Maryland Room, C. Burr Artz Public Library, Frederick County Public Libraries.

11. Mittelberger, 119.

12. Otto Hively, "Pennsylvania Original Land Records, Series for York County," https://www.yorkhistorycenter.org/wp-content/uploads/2016/05/1-PENNSYLVANIA-ORIGINAL-LAND-RECORDS.pdf.

Chapter 5. Opportunity in Maryland

1. Paula S. Reed, *Tillers of the Soil: A History of Agriculture in Mid-Maryland* (Frederick: Catoctin Center for Regional Studies, 2011), 4.

2. Reed, *Tillers of the Soil*, 5. Also: Frank W. Porter III, "From Backcountry to County: The Delayed Settlement of Western Maryland," *Maryland Historical Magazine*, Winter 1975, 329-349, MSA SC 5881-1-280.

3. Archives of Maryland Online (AOMOL), vol. 28, pp. 25-26, Maryland State Archives (MSA).

4. Reed, 5.

5. Robert J. Brugger, *Maryland, A Middle Temperament, 1634-1980* (Baltimore: The Johns Hopkins University Press, 1988), 67-68.

6. Hettie L. Ballweber, *"History and Archaeology at the Schifferstadt Site (18FR134), Frederick, Maryland"* contrib. Lori Frye, Justine McKnight, Edward Otter, Paula Mask and Eric Jenkins (Columbia: ACS Consultants, 1997), [for Frederick County Landmarks Foundation], 269. A copy of this report can be viewed at Heritage Frederick, Frederick, MD.

7. Timothy Silver, *A New Face on the Countryside: Indians, Colonists and Slaves in South Atlantic Forests, 1500-1800* (Cambridge: Cambridge University Press, 1990), 26.

8. Dennis Curry, "Heater's Island and the Piscataway Indians," *Our History, Our Heritage* (blog), The Maryland Historical Trust, April 24, 2015, https://mdhistoricaltrust.wordpress.com/2015/04/24/heaters-island-piscataway/.

9. Abdel Ross Wentz, *History of the Evangelical Lutheran Church of Frederick, Maryland, 1738-1938* (Harrisburg: Evangelical Press, 1938),70, https://hdl.handle.net/2027/wu.89072975881.

10. "Frederick Town" is used in this work. This version of the town's name was used consistently in documents found in the Maryland Archives and in early legal documents such as deeds and wills. It's also listed in this form on the first map of the city drawn by Samuel Duvall in 1782. A copy of the map can be viewed on the "Maryland

Historical Mapping" website:
https://msa.maryland.gov/megafile/msa/stagsere/se1/se34/000100/
000143/pdf/se34-143.pdf.

Chapter 6. A New Brunner Home

1. Abby Holtz, "Schiefferstadt Stone House of Frederick, Maryland" (New Market: Abby Holtz, n.d.), 8.

2. Samuel Kercheval, *A History of the Valley of Virginia* (Winchester: Samuel H. Davis, 1833), 355-357, https://archive.org/stream/ahistoryvalleyv01jacogoog#page/n6.

3. Prince George's County Court (Land Records) (PGCCLR), 1743-1746, Clerk BB, Book 1/page 444, MSA CE 65-12. Note: Quantity 303 acres. This and the next three deeds are dated July 28, 1746.

4. PGCCLR, 1743-1746, BB 1/441, MSA CE 65-12. Quantity: 186.25 acres.

5. PGCCLR, 1743-1746, BB 1/442, MSA CE 65-12. Quantity: 232.25 acres.

6. PGCCLR, 1743-1746, BB 1/432, MSA CE 65-12. Quantity: 248 acres.

7. Tracey and Dern, *Pioneers of Old Monocacy*, 160. Note: Getzendanner's land was received through a patent on November 11, 1742 for 100 acres. Patent LG B:533.

8. PGCCLR, 1743-1746, BB 1/437, MSA CE 65-12. Quantity: 473 acres, deed dated July 28, 1746.

9. Frederick County Court Land Records (FCCLR), 1752-1756, Book E/page 278, MSA CE 108-2. Quantity: 307.25 acres, deed dated September 25, 1753.

10. "Mutual Insurance Policy #467," November 10, 1848, Frederick County Landmarks Foundation. A transcription of this document is found in Ballweber, *History and Archaeology at the Schifferstadt Site*, vol. 2, Appendix IV. Courtesy of the Frederick County Landmarks Foundation.

11. Ballweber, *History and Archaeology at the Schifferstadt Site*, 38. As a result of the expansion of Maryland Route 15 in the 1960s,

Carroll Creek was moved "240 feet south
of its original channel."

12. Ballweber, 269.

13. K. Edward Lay, "European Antecedents of Seventeenth and Eighteenth Century
Germanic and Scots-Irish Architecture in America," *Pennsylvania Folklife Magazine*,
Autumn 1982, 2-43, https://digitalcommons.ursinus.edu/pafolklifemag/98.

14. PGCCLR, 1743-1746, BB 1/444, MSA CE 65-12.

15. Lucy Forney Bittinger, *The Germans in Colonial Times* (Philadelphia and London: J. B. Lippincott Company, 1901), 119, https://archive.org/details/germansincolonia00inbitt/page/n5. Also: Rush, *An Account of the Manners*, 66.

16. Frederick County Government (FCG), Register of Wills, Frederick County, Maryland (ROWFCM), Liber GM, No.1/folio 44, Wills 1777-1784, December 24, 1775.

17. FCG, ROWFCM, A 1/564, Wills 1744-1777, February 15, 1776.

18. John G. Gagliardo, "Germans and Agriculture in Colonial Pennsylvania," *The Pennsylvania Magazine of History and Biography*, April 1959, 192-218, https://journals.psu.edu/pmhb/article/view/41466/41187.

19. Stevenson Whitcomb Fletcher, *Pennsylvania Agriculture and Country Life 1640-1840* (Harrisburg: Commonwealth of Pennsylvania, Pennsylvania Historical and Museum
Commission, 1950), 69, https://hdl.handle.net/2027/mdp.39015020104371.

20. Irwin Richman, *German Architecture in America: Folk House, Your House, Bauhaus, and More* (Atglen: Schiffer Publishing Ltd., 2003), 36.

21. Tracey and Dern, 129. Also: Paula S. Reed and Edith B. Wallace, *Monocacy National
Battlefield: Cultural Resources Study* (Hagerstown: for the U S Government, 1999), 11.

22. "The Dulany Family Papers, 1727-1786," *The Historical Society*

of Frederick County Archives and Research Center, MS0001, (blog), May 18, 2013, https://hsfrederickco.wordpress.com/finding-aids-2/ms0001-the-dulany-family-papers- 1727-1786/.

23. *The Calvert Papers, Number Two, Selections from Correspondence, Fund Publication No. 34* (Baltimore: Maryland Historical Society,1894), 116, https://archive.org/details/calvertpapers02leej/page/n7.

24. AOMOL, vol. 700, pp. 28-31, MSA, https://msa.maryland.gov/megafile/msa/speccol/sc2900/sc2908/000001/000700/html/am700—28.html.

25. Porter, *From Backcountry to County*, 344.

26. Thomas J.C. Williams and Folger McKinsey, *History of Frederick County, Maryland, from the Earliest Settlements to the Beginning of the War between the States,* vol. 1 (Frederick: L.R. Titsworth & Company, 1910), 24, https://hdl.handle.net/2027/chi.22614837.

27. AOMOL, vol. 700, pp. 28-32, MSA.

28. Beverley W. Bond, Jr, "The Quit-Rent System in the American Colonies," *The American Historical Review*, April 1912, 500, https://www.jstor.org/stable/1834386.

29. Williams and McKinsey, *History of Frederick County*, 24.

30. Klaus Wust, *Johann Thomas Schley (1712-1790) Schoolmaster, Musician and Fraktur Artist of Frederick, Maryland* (Baltimore: Society for the History of the Germans in Maryland, 1993), 81-89, https://loyolanotredamelib.org/php/report05/articles/pdfs/report42Wust81-89.pdf.

31. "The Schley Family Papers," *The Historical Society of Frederick County Archives and Research Center* (blog), MS0008, May 8, 2013, https://hsfrederickco.wordpress.com/finding-aids-2/ms0008-the-schley-family-papers/.

32. Henry Harbaugh, Rev. A.M., *The Life of Rev. Michael Schlatter; with a Full Account of His Travels and Labors among the Germans in Pennsylvania, New Jersey, Maryland and Virginia; Including His Services as Chaplain in the French and Indian War, and in the War of the Revolution. 1716 to 1790* (Philadelphia: Lindsay & Blakiston,

1857), 177, https://archive.org/details/lifeofrevmichael00harba.

33. "The Schley Family Papers MS0008" (blog).

34. James DiLisio, *Maryland Geography: An Introduction* (Baltimore: Johns Hopkins University Press, 2014), 23.

35. Winthrop Sargent, *The History of an Expedition against Fort Du Quesne, in 1755; under Major-General Edward Braddock* (Philadelphia: J. B. Lippincott, 1856), 368, https://archive.org/details/historyofexpedit00sarg.

36. Charlotte Browne, "Charlotte Browne Diary, 1754-1757, 1763-1766," *New-York Historical Society*, 53. Item ID: Nyhs_cbd_p-51.Jpgnyhs_cb," https://cdm16694.contentdm.oclc.org/digital/collection/p16124coll1/id/9876/rec/1.

37. No records of the marriage or of Albertina's maiden name have been found.

38. FCCLR, 1752-1756, E/68, MSA CE 108-2.

39. James Byrne Ranck et al., *A History of the Evangelical Reformed Church, Frederick, Maryland:"Unto Us..."* (Frederick: [n.p.], 1964), Appendix II, 190. Joseph was listed as "Eltester" translated as "Elder," on his son Jacob's church marriage record in German in 1725: Johnson, *Kinfolk in Germany*, 26-27.

40. William J. Hinke, Ph. D. trans., Frederick S. Weiser ed., *Maryland German Church Records: Records of the Evangelical Reformed Church (a congregation of the United Church of Christ) Frederick, Frederick County, Maryland, 1746-1789* (Westminster: Historical Society of Carroll County, 1991), 2, 4, 16, 18. Stephan was baptized on 7 May, 1749, date of birth not given. Johann Peter was born on 31 March, 1753, date of baptism not given. Johannes was baptized on 21 October, 1759, date of birth not given. It is reasonable to assume that this child was deceased at the time a second son named Johannes was born on 21 June, 1761 and baptized 2 August, 1761. Neither of the two younger sons were listed in Elias' will dated 1783.

Chapter 7. Brunners on the Record, Part 1

1. Prince George's County Court (Levy Book), 1734-1794, 64, 207, MSA C1245-1, MdHR 6177.

2. A Marylander, *Dulany's History of Maryland, from 1632 to 1891, Prepared for the Use of Schools in the State* (Baltimore: Wm. J. C. Dulany Company, 1891), 110-111, https://archive.org/stream/dulanyshistoryof00saff##page/n3/.

3. Prince George's County Court (Levy Book), 03/1738-06/1740, pp. 506, 567, 661, C1191-16, MdHR 5759, MSA.

4. Jeffrey A. Wyand and Florence L. Wyand, *Colonial Maryland Naturalizations* (Baltimore: Genealogical Publishing Co., Inc., 1975), v-vii. Also, "Commission Book, 82," *Maryland Historical Magazine*, June 1931, 138-158, MSA SC 5881-1-102. The family name appears as "Branner" in these records and only the names of the men and children are listed.

5. Tracey and Dern, 272. The law stated "All Public Main Roads shall be well grubbed, fit for travelling, Twenty Feet wide; and good substantial Bridges made over all Heads of Rivers, Creeks, Branches and Swamps." Overseers were appointed every year by the county court and were fined if their duties were neglected. AOMOL, vol. 75, p. 671, MSA.

6. Tracey and Dern, 96.

7. Tracey and Dern, 371.

8. AOMOL, vol. 46, pp. 142-146, MSA.

9. Cunz, *The Maryland Germans*, 67-68.

10. FCCLR, 1763-1767, J/362, MSA CE 108-6. The original land records were said to have conveyed title of Lot 82 for the use of the congregation. In an 1809 session law, the parcel was corrected to Lot 80: AOMOL, vol. 570, pp. 21-22, MSA.

11. "Trinity Chapel, 1763/1881" (Published in honor of Dorothy S. and James B. Ranck, faithful historians of Evangelical Reformed Church, 1988),pamphlet. Note: the congregation was given an allowance for use of the "Dutch Meeting House" in June, 1750 as payment for "keeping court" there, while the permanent courthouse

building was under construction: Millard Milburn Rice, *This Was the Life* (Baltimore: Genealogical Publishing Co., Inc., 1984), 43.

12. Ranck et al., *A History of the Evangelical Reformed Church*, 16.

13. Harbaugh, *The Life of Rev. Michael Schlatter*, 171, 176, https://archive.org/details/lifeofrevmichael00harb.

14. H. Austin Cooper, Rev., A Pleasant View (Burkittsville: Pleasant View Church of the Brethren, 1998), 407.

15. AOMOL, vol. 28, pp. 420-424, MSA.

16. Rice, *This Was the Life*, 59.

17. Cunz, 70.

18. AOMOL, vol. 75, pp. 508-509, MSA.

19. FCCLR, 1748-1752, B/415, MSA CE 108-1.

20. FCCLR, 1752-1756, E/104, MSA CE 108-2.

21. Ranck et al., 185-186, 191.

22. Harbaugh, 171.

23. John Philip Boehm, Rev., *Minutes and Letters of the Coetus of the German Reformed Congregations in Pennsylvania 1747-1792* (Philadelphia: Reformed Church Publication Board, 1903), 199, https://archive.org/stream/minuteslettersof00refo#page/n5/mode/2up. Note: In 1761, the Frederick Reformed congregation school was "attended by 40 children." The number of families in the congregation was 80 at that time.

24. Harbaugh, 258.

25. AOMOL, vol. 14, p. 115, MSA.

26. AOMOL, vol. 75, p. 641, MSA.

27. Williams and McKinsey, 521. Also: Bernard C. Steiner, Ph.D., *History of Education in Maryland* (Washington: Government Printing Office, 1894), 41-42, https://babel.hathitrust.org/cgi/pt?id=mdp.39015070175909;view=1up;seq=7.

Chapter 8. War Terrorizes a Peaceful Valley

1. Joseph Banvard, *Tragic Scenes in the History of Maryland and*

the Old French War: With an Account of Various Interesting Contemporaneous Events Which Occurred in the Early Settlement of America (Boston: Gould and Lincoln, 1856), 143-144, https://archive.org/details/tragicscenes00banvrich/page/n13.

2. *The French and Indian War: 1754-1763*, Teacher's Education Kit, 30, https://www.nps.gov/common/uploads/teachers/lessonplans/FI%20teacher%20background3.pdf.

3. Charles Morse Stotz, "Defense in the Wilderness," *The Western Pennsylvania Historical Magazine*, November 1958, 62, https://journals.psu.edu/wph/article/view/2619/2452.

4. Banvard, *Tragic Scenes in the History of Maryland*, 144.

5. Newton Dennison Mereness, *Maryland as a Proprietary Province* (New York: The Macmillan Company, 1901), 317, https://archive.org/details/marylandaspropri00mererich/page/n8.

6. "Annapolis: Extract of a Letter from a Gentleman in Virginia to his Friend Here, dated January 16," *Maryland Gazette*, February 14, 1754, 2, MSA SC 2731, M1279.

7. George Washington, *The Writings of George Washington: Being His Correspondence, Addresses, Messages, and Other Papers, Official and Private, Selected and Published from the Manuscripts, with a Life of the Author*, notes and illustr. Jared Sparks, vol. 1 (Boston: Ferdinand Andrews, 1839), 41-42, https://hdl.handle.net/2027/nyp.33433112148394.

8. William Hand Browne, *Maryland; the History of a Palatinate* (Boston: Houghton Mifflin Company, 1884), 220-221, https://hdl.handle.net/2027/uc2.ark:/13960/t1zc82r84.

9. Washington, *The Writings of George Washington*, 43.

10. "An impartial and succinct History of the origin and progress of the present War," *The London Magazine or Gentlemen's Monthly Intelligencer*, vol. 28, September 1759, 459, https://hdl.handle.net/2027/mdp.39015006991296.

11. Sargent, *The History of an Expedition*, 368.

12. James M. Perry, *Arrogant Armies: Great Military Disasters and the Generals Behind Them* (Edison: Castle Books, 2005), 11.

13. Benjamin Franklin, *The Autobiography of Benjamin Franklin*,

ed. John Bigelow (New York and London: G. P. Putnam's Sons, 1890), 240, https://archive.org/details/autobiographybe00bigegoog.

14. Franklin, *The Autobiography of Benjamin Franklin*, 241.

15. Franklin, 246-247.

16. Alan Houston, "Benjamin Franklin and the 'Wagon Affair' of 1755," *The William and Mary Quarterly*, April 2009, 271-272.

17. Sargent, 232.

18. Mereness, *Maryland as a Proprietary Province*, 308.

19. *Maryland Gazette*, April 1, 1756,1-2, MSA SC 2731, M1279.

20. George Washington, *The Writings of George Washington: Being His Correspondence, Addresses, Messages, and Other Papers, Official and Private, Selected and Published from the Original Manuscripts / with a Life of the Author*, notes and illustr. Jared Sparks, vol. 2 (Boston: Russell, Odiorne, and Metcalf, and Hilliard, Gray, and Co., 1833), 183, https://hdl.handle.net/2027/hvd.hwb4dk. Note: Washington may have used the name "Monocacy" here to distinguish Frederick Town, Maryland from Winchester, Virginia, also named Frederick Town, from 1738 until 1752.

21. "Annapolis, August 4," *Maryland Gazette*, August 4, 1757, 3, MSA SC 2731, M1279.

22. AOMOL, vol. 9, p. 57, MSA.

23. "French and Indian War," *Maryland Historical Magazine*, 354-356, December 1914, MSA SC 5881-1-36 . This source also shows, on page 367, that Stephen Ransberger and John Bruner were owed money for unspecified supplies they provided to the militia.

24. AOMOL, vol. 9, p. 70, MSA.

25. "To the Governor of Maryland," *Maryland Gazette*, May 12, 1757, 3, MSA SC 2731, M1279. This is a letter to Governor Sharpe from the Cherokee Chief at Fort Frederick.

26. "Charles-Town," *Maryland Gazette*, June 30, 1757, 2, MSA SC 2731, M1279.

27. "Williamsburg, May 6," *Maryland Gazette*, May 19, 1757, 2, MSA SC 2731, M1279.

28. AOMOL, vol. 55, pp. 315-319, MSA.

29. AOMOL, vol. 44, pg. 697, MSA.

30. Mereness, 317.

31. "Reassignment of Journal Allowance," 3/24/1767, MSA S1005-73-9854, MdHR 19,999-068-261.

32. David Curtis Skaggs, "Maryland's Impulse Toward Social Revolution: 1750-1776," *The Journal of America History*, March 1968, 776, https://www.jstor.org/stable/1918069.

Chapter 9. Brunners on the Record—Part 2

1. "Annapolis, April 22," *Maryland Gazette*, April 22, 1762, 3, MSA SC2731, M1280.

2. State of Maryland, *Calendar of Maryland State Papers No. 1: The Black Books* (Annapolis: Publications of The Hall of Records Commission No. 1, 1943), 174-175, 1205 I, I and 1206 III, 42.

3. AOMOL, vol. 32, pp. 37-38, MSA.

4. J. Thomas Scharf, A.M., *History of Western Maryland: Being a History of Frederick, Montgomery, Carroll, Washington, Allegany, and Garrett Counties from the Earliest Period to the Present Day/ ; Including Biographical Sketches of Their Representative Men*, vol. 1 of 2 (Philadelphia: Louis H. Everts, 1882),121, https://archive.org/details/historyofwestern01scha/page/n7.

5. Scharf, History of Western Maryland, 121.

6. Rice, 273.

7. Scharf, 122-123.

8. Bernard Christian Steiner, *Western Maryland in the Revolution* (Baltimore: Johns Hopkins Press, 1902), 7, https://archive.org/details/westernmarylandi00stei/page/n5.

9. Steiner, *Western Maryland in the Revolution*, 13-14.

10. Nead, The Pennsylvania-German, 188-190.

11. AOMOL, vol. 18, p. 50, MSA.

12. AOMOL, vol. 18, p 47, MSA.

13. Andrew Krug, "'Such a Banndity You Never See Collected!': Frederick Town and the American Revolution," *Maryland Historical Magazine*, Spring 2000, 16, MSA SC5881-1-378, citing AOMOL, vol. 45, pp. 16, 46, 94, 139, MSA.

14. Steiner, Revolution, 49.

15. Cunz, 149-150.

16. Johann Conrad Döhla, *A Hessian Diary of the American Revolution*, trans., ed. and intro. Bruce Burgoyne (Norman and London: University of Oklahoma Press, 1990), 220.

17. William MacDonald, *Select documents illustrative of the history of the United States, 1776-1861* (New York; London: Macmillan, 1905), 7, https://archive.org/details/selectdocuments00macdrich/page/6.

18. Williams and McKinsey, 267.

19. Julian Ursyn Niemcewicz, *Under Their Vine and Fig Tree*, trans., ed., intro. and notes Metchie J. E. Budka (Elizabeth: The Grassman Publishing Co., Inc., 1965), 113.

20. Jedidiah Morse, *The American Universal Geography; or, A View of the Present State of All the Kingdoms, States and Colonies in the New World*, part first, fifth edition (Boston: Thomas & Andrews, 1805), 601, https://hdl.handle.net/2027/hvd.hxj3rz.

21. FCG, ROWFCM, GM 1/44, Wills 1777-1784, December 24, 1775.

22. FCG, ROWFCM, A 1/564, Wills 1744-1777, February 15, 1776.

23. FCG, ROWFCM, GM 2/7, Wills 1783-1794, October 14, 1783.

Chapter 10. A Year at Schifferstadt

1. General colonial farming information used in this chapter can be found in: Stevenson Whitcomb Fletcher, *Pennsylvania Agriculture and Country Life 1640-1840* (Harrisburg: Commonwealth of Pennsylvania, Pennsylvania Historical and Museum Commission, 1950), https://hdl.handle.net/2027/mdp.39015020104371. Also: John G. Gagliardo, "Germans and Agriculture in Colonial Pennsylvania," *The Pennsylvania Magazine of History and Biography*, April 1959, 192-218, https://journals.psu.edu/pmhb/article/view/41466/41187.

2. Alan G. Keyser, "Gardens and Gardening Among the Pennsylvania Germans," *Pennsylvania Folklife Magazine*, Spring 1971, 2-15, https://digitalcommons.ursinus.edu/pafolklifemag/44.

3. Edwin Miller Fogel, Ph.D., *Beliefs and Superstitions of the Pennsylvania Germans* (Philadelphia: American Germanica Press, 1915), 206, https://archive.org/details/superstitionpenn00fogerich.

4. Fogel, *Beliefs and Superstitions*, 196-197.

5. Fogel, 206-207.

6. FCCLR, 1752-1756, E/48, MSA CE 108-2. On January 1, 1753, the Brunner brothers recorded the marks of their cattle and hogs at the courthouse as follows: Jacob: "A Crop off the Left Ear and a half Crop off the Right Ear"; John: "A Crop off the Left Ear and a Slit and a half penny [a circular hole] out of the Right"; Henry: "A Crop off the Right Ear and a Slit in the Left Ear"; Elias: "A Crop off the Left Ear."

7. Ellen J. Gehret and Alan G. Keyser, "Flax Processing in Pennsylvania: From Seed to Fiber," *Pennsylvania Folklife Magazine*, Autumn 1972, 10-34, https://digitalcommons.ursinus.edu/pafolklifemag/51.

8. Arthur Pierce Middleton, Ph.D., *Tobacco Coast, A Maritime History of Chesapeake Bay in the Colonial Era*, ed. George Carrington Mason (Newport News: The Mariners' Museum, 1953), 124.

9. Dr. Henry Miller, "The Lure of Sotweed: Tobacco and Maryland History," *Historic St. Mary's City*, n.d., https://www.hsmcdigshistory.org/pdf/Tobacco.pdf.

10. Mabel Snyder, "How I Make Soap," *Pennsylvania Folklife Magazine*, Summer 1968, 12-15, https://digitalcommons.ursinus.edu/pafolklifemag/33.

11. Amy Lee Huffman Reed and Marie LaForge Burns, *In and Out of Frederick Town: Colonial Occupations*, illustr. Judith Proffitt (Frederick: n.p., 1985), 34-43.

12. Ellen J. Gehret, Janet Gray Crosson tech. ed. *Rural Pennsylvania Clothing, Being a Study of the Wearing Apparel of the German and English Inhabitants Both Men and Women Who Resided in Southeastern Pennsylvania in the Late Eighteenth and Early Nineteenth Century* (York: Liberty Cap Books, 1976), 73.

13. AOMOL, vol. 13, pp. 425-430, MSA.

14. Trinity Chapel brochure.

15. Donald Graves and Michael Colby, "An Overview of Flax and Linen Production in Pennsylvania," *Pennsylvania Folklife Magazine*,

Spring 1986, 108-126, https://digitalcommons.ursinus.edu/pafolklifemag/112.

16. Don Yoder, "SAUERKRAUT in the Pennsylvania Folk-Culture," *Pennsylvania Folklife Magazine*, Summer 1961, 56-69, https://digitalcommons.ursinus.edu/pafolklifemag/11.

17. Ed Kraus, "How to Make Applejack," n.d., https://eckraus.com/how-to-make-applejack/.

18. ERIC, ED304351: Historic Pennsylvania Leaflets No. 1-41. 1960-1988 (Harrisburg: Pennsylvania State Historical and Museum Commission, 1988), 15-18, https://archive.org/details/ERIC_ED304351.

19. "Advertisements," *Maryland Gazette*, September 1, 1747, 3, MSA SC M1278, p. 549. "All Persons who will bring any Goods, Merchandizes [sic], Cattle, or any Thing else to the said Fairs, or Markets, to sell, shall be free and exempt from the Payment of any Toll, Stallage, Piccage, or any other Charge, for the Term of Five Years next ensuing this last day of August 1747. D. Dulany."

20. "Tuskarora Glass Works 4 Miles North of Frederickstown Maryland 1752," *Historical American Glass* (blog), n.d., http://historical-american-glass.com/tuskarora-glass-works-4-miles-north-of-frederickstown-maryland-1752.html.

21. James Curtis Ballagh, *The South in the Building of the Nation*, vol. 5 (Richmond: The Southern Historical Publication Society, 1909), 581, https://hdl.handle.net/2027/nyp.33433081790184.

22. Alfred L. Shoemaker, "Belsnickel Lore," *Pennsylvania Folklife Magazine*, Spring 1997, 109-112, https://digitalcommons.ursinus.edu/pafolklifemag/150.

23. Theodore Baker trans, "'Es Ist Ein Ros Entsprungen' – 'Lo, How a Rose E'er Blooming'," *The German Way & More, Language in Germany, Austria and Switzerland* (blog), n.d., https://www.german-way.com/history-and-culture/german-language/german-christmas-carols/es-ist-ein-ros-entsprungen-lo-how-a-rose-eer-blooming/. This hymn "appeared in the Speyer hymnal, printed in Cologne in 1599."

24. Sue Bowman, "Lime a Staple of Life in Earlier Times," *Lancaster Farming* (blog), June 3, 2012, https://

www.lancasterfarming.com/news/main_edition/lime-a-staple-of-life-in-earlier-times/article_c793e64c-b02b-5bd9-bbf0-49da8ff4bfca.html.

Chapter 11. Schifferstadt Over the Centuries

1. PGCCLR, 1743-1746, BB 1/444, MSA CE 65-12.
2. FCCLR,1752-1756, E/68, MSA CE 108-2.
3. FCCLR, 1771-1771, O/136, MSA CE 108-11. It is assumed that Elias and his family moved to Frederick Town. Elias owned lot number 269: FCCLR K/499, May 20, 1766, MSA CE 108-7. Note: Records indicate that Christopher (known as Stoffel) Meyer signed personal bonds to be paid annually to Elias Brunner for the purchase of Schifferstadt. In effect, Elias held the mortgage to the farm, as Christopher paid it off over time. These bonds date from 1770 to 1777, totaling the £1,600 purchase price. Photocopies of the bonds are in the files of The Maryland Room, C. Burr Artz Library, Frederick County Public Libraries, file MR-9-1-6, Brunner, Elias. Also: Meyer married Stephen Ramsburgh's daughter, Anna Margaret. She is the granddaughter of Joseph, the now deceased patriarch. Stephen had married Joseph's daughter, Maria Catherine. See: Lewis H. Steiner, M.D. and Bernard C. Steiner, Ph. D., *The Genealogy of the Steiner Family, Especially of the Descendants of Jacob Steiner* (Baltimore: Press of the Friedenwald Co., 1896), 36-37, https://archive.org/details/genealogyofstein00stei.
4. Special Collections (Chancery Court Abstracts), 21 Jun 1782, "Baker Johnson vs. Christopher Mayer, Contract to Purchase," MSA S512-2915, MdHR 17898-2835, https://msa.maryland.gov/msa/speccol/sc6000/sc6016/county/frederick/chancery/2835.htm. In his will recorded on July 1, 1811, Baker Johnson bequeaths to his son Charles "my Mount Airy farm." No boundaries are listed for this farm, but later public records will refer to the 125 acre parcel by this name: MSA, MARYLAND REGISTER OF WILLS Records, 1629-1999," images, FamilySearch (https://familysearch.org/ark:/61903/3:1:33SQ-GT1V-9TV?cc=1803986&wc=SNYH-

BZS%3A146535301%2C147326301 : 20 May 2014) accessed 9/17/ 2018, Frederick > Wills 1809-1815 vol 1 > image 104 of 310; Hall of Records, Annapolis.

5. FCG, ROWFCM,1809-1815, RB 1/518, March 20, 1812.

6. FCG, ROWFCM, 1815-1817, HS 2/11, June 19, 1815. Administration Bonds (not Wills).

7. FCCLR, 1820-1821, JS 12/ 273, MSA CE108-80.

8. FCG, ROWFCM, 1822-1828, HS 3/261, January 17, 1824.

9. FCCLR, 1828-1829, JS 30/157, MSA CE 108-98.

10. FCG, ROWFCM, 1834 to 1843, GME 2/680, March 10, 1842.

11. FCCLR, 1842-1843, HS 17/501, MSA CE 108-135.

12. Steiner and Steiner, *The Genealogy of the Steiner Family*, 36.

13. FCCLR, 1843-1844, HS 19/ 287, MSA CE 108-137.

14. "United States Census, 1850," database with images, FamilySearch(https://familysearch.org/ark:/61903/1:1:MD4F-XCG : 12 April 2016), Martin Yonson in household of Henry Yonson, Fredericktown, Frederick, Maryland, United States; citing family 402, NARA microfilm publication M432 (Washington, D.C.: National Archives and Records Administration, n.d.).
"United States Census, 1860", database with images, FamilySearch(https://familysearch.org/ark:/61903/1:1:M69C-5CY : 12 December 2017), Martin Yenson, 1860.
"United States Census, 1870," database with images, FamilySearch (https://familysearch.org/ark:/61903/3:1:S3HT-67F3-R7N?cc=1438024&wc=92KH-PT5%3A518652801%2C519195401%2C518655601 : 22 May 2014), Maryland > Frederick > District 2 > image 6 of 87; citing NARA microfilm publication M593 (Washington, D.C.: National Archives and Records Administration, n.d.).

15. FCG, ROWFCM, 1860-1865 vol. 15, APK 1/154. Will was dated October 15, 1855 and probated on February 24, 1862.

16. Steiner and Steiner, 54-56.

17. Dr. Lewis H. Steiner died on February 18, 1892 without a will. This fact is included in the deed dated December 26, 1899, in which

his heirs sell the "Schieverstadt" property to Edward C. Krantz.

18. FCCLR, 1899-1900, DHH 5/447, MSA CE 61-95.

19. FCCLR, 1900-1900, EGH 358/227, MSA CE 61-203.

20. FCCLR, 1926-1927, EGH 360/355, MSA CE 61-205.

21. Find a Grave, Frederick Biser Krantz, https://www.findagrave.com/memorial/24453607/bessie-c-krantz.

22. FCCLR, 1958-1958, ECW 595/310, MSA CE 61-440.

23. FCCLR, 1963-1963, ECW 688/385, MSA CE 61-533.

24. Find A Grave, Bessie C. Krantz, https://www.findagrave.com/memorial/24453607/bessie-c-krantz, accessed 9/17/2018.

25. FCCLR, 1974-1974, ECW 943/89, MSA CE 61-788.

26. "Schifferstadt Title Taken By Landmarks Foundation," *The News*, July 2, 1974, 1, on microfilm at The Maryland Room, C. Burr Artz Public Library, Frederick County Public Libraries.

27. John D. Milner, AIA, *Schiefferstadt: A Restoration Study, with contributions by Allan H. Steenhusen, Jeffrey C. Bourke and Alice Kent Schooler* (West Chester: National Heritage Corporation, December 1974), [for Frederick County Landmarks Foundation, Incorporated]. Courtesy of the Frederick County Landmarks Foundation.

28. Ballweber.

29. Karen Gardner, "Schifferstadt Shows Its Age," *The Frederick News-Post*, August 26, 1994, B1, B3, on microfilm at The Maryland Room, C. Burr Artz Public Library, Frederick County Public Libraries.

Chapter 12. Schifferstadt Architectural Museum

1. Kristie Baynard, *National Register of Historic Places, Schifferstadt, Frederick, Maryland, National Register # NL100000833, USDI/NPS NRHP Registration Form*, (Washington, DC: for the U.S. Department of the Interior, National Park Service, March 8, 2016), 27. Also: extensive on-site observations by co-author Boyce Rensberger. Note: Author's surname is misspelled as "Bayard" on the report.

2. Stephanie Griffith, "Germany Rediscovers an Honored Style," *The New York Times*, November 3, 1988, 14, https://www.nytimes.com/

1988/11/03/garden/germany-rediscovers-an-honored-style.html.

3. Milner, *Schiefferstadt: A Restoration Study*, 22.

4. Cynthia G. Falk, *Architecture and Artifacts of the Pennsylvania Germans* (University Park: The Pennsylvania State University Press, 2008), 61.

5. Richman, *German Architecture in America*, 34.

6. Williams and McKinsey, 9-10.

7. Baynard, "National Register of Historic Places," 4.

8. Kenneth R. LeVan, *Building Construction and Materials of the Pennsylvania Germans. A Basic Introduction to the Most Common Construction Techniques and Decorative Features of Early Pennsylvania German Buildings* (Harrisburg: Vernacular Architecture Forum Annual Meeting, 2004), 20.

9. G. Edwin Brumbaugh, *Colonial Architecture of the Pennsylvania Germans. Originally Delivered as an Address before the Forty-First Meeting of the Pennsylvania German Society at Reading* (Lancaster: Pennsylvania German Society, 1931), 55-56, https://archive.org/details/pennsylvaniagerm02penn_1/page/n53.

10. LeVan, *Building Construction and Materials*, 20.

11. LeVan, 20.

12. Ballweber, 59.

13. "Mutual Insurance Policy #467." Also: Milner, 19.

14. Milner, 19.

15. Milner, 28.

16. Baynard, 4.

17. LeVan, 33.

18. Milner, 18.

19. LeVan, 13.

20. Brumbaugh, *Colonial Architecture of the Pennsylvania Germans*, 24 and Plate 4.

21. J. Richard Rivoire, "National Register of Historic Places Inventory-Nomination Form," August 25, 1973, 1. This form can be found in the files of the *Maryland Historical Trust*, Maryland Inventory of Historic Properties, inventory no. F-3-47, https://mht.maryland.gov/

mihp/MIHPCard.aspx?MIHPNo=F-3-47.

22. William Woys Weaver, "The Pennsylvania German House: European Antecedents and New World Forms," *Winterthur Portfolio*, Winter 1986, 253, http://www.jstor.org/stable/1181052.

23. Falk, *Architecture and Artifacts*, 25.

24. Sally McMurry and Nancy Van Dolsen eds., *Architecture and Landscape of the Pennsylvania Germans, 1720-1920* (Philadelphia and Oxford: University of Pennsylvania Press, 2011), 39.

25. Brumbaugh, 29.

26. Weaver, "The Pennsylvania German House," 258.

27. LeVan, 32.

28. "Tuskarora Glass Works," *Historical American Glass*.

29. Milner, 37.

30. Lay, "European Antecedents of the Seventeenth," 21, figure 4.

31. Intro. Ellen Gehret and Alan Keyser, *The Homespun Textile Tradition of the Pennsylvania Germans*, exihibition catalogue (Lancaster: Pennsylvania Farm Museum of Landis Valley, 1976), 28, https://archive.org/details/homespuntextilet00unse/page/n3.

32. McMurry and Van Dolsen, *Architecture and Landscape*, 35.

33. Brumbaugh, Plate 38.

34. Milner, 26.

35. Lay, 25-26.

36. Milner, 27.

37. Milner, 24.

38. Milner, Illustration # 10.

39. Rivoire, "National Register of Historic Places," 5.

40. Milner, 32. The partition may have been added after original construction.

41. Baynard, 6.

42. Henry C. Mercer, *The Bible in Iron or The Pictured Stoves and Stove Plates of the Pennsylvania Germans* (Doylestown: Bucks County Historical Society, 1914), Chapter 1, https://archive.org/details/bibleiniron01merc/page/n5.

43. Rush, 60.

44. "Archaeological and Historical Analysis: Pennsylvania Colonial

Iron Production at Elizabeth Furnace," n.d., *Millersville University*, https://www.millersville.edu/archaeology/research/elizabeth-furnace/analysis.php.

45. Milner, 49.

46. Rush, 85-86.

47. "Mutual Insurance Policy".

48. Robert C. Bucher, "Grain in the Attic," *Pennsylvania Folklife Magazine*, Winter 1962-63, 7-15, https://digitalcommons.ursinus.edu/pafolklifemag/15.

49. Bucher, "Grain in the Attic," 14-15.

50. Baynard, 15.

51. "Mutual Insurance Policy,"

52. Ballweber, 102-103.

53. Richard H. Shaner, "Outdoor Ovens in the Dutch Country," *Pennsylvania Folklife Magazine*, Summer 1981, 6-7, https://digitalcommons.ursinus.edu/pafolklifemag/93.

54. Patricia L. Faust, "Firing a Bake Oven," *Early American Life Magazine*, October 1977, 48-49.

ILLUSTRATION NOTES

We must thank the anonymous artists who created the illustrations used in this book. A few are "artist's conceptions" based as much on imagination as on evidence. Nonetheless they show how people a century or so ago thought about the events depicted. Artwork in Chapter 10 is factually based. It was designed by H. L. Fischer and drawn by Henry Barratt. It was first published in 1879 in *Die Alte 'Zeite* (Olden Times) by H.L. Fischer. All these images, thankfully, are out of copyright.

Page 3: Adapted from William Beidelman, *The Story of the Pennsylvania Germans, Embracing an Account of Their Origin, Their History and Their Dialect* (Easton: Express Book Print, 1898), frontispiece.

Page 5: Lionel Pincus and Princess Firyal Map Division, The New York Public Library. "Carte particulìere des pays quì sont sìtuéz entre la Rhein, la Saare, la Mosselle et la basse Alsace, contenant partìe du Palatinat, des Electorats de Mayence de Treves des Eveschés de Spìre et de Wormes avec les Duchés de Deuxponts et des Sìmmeren." New York Public Library Digital Collections. http://digitalcollections.nypl.org/items/510d47e4-1cdf-a3d9-e040-e00a18064a99.

Page 8: "An engraved vintage illustration portrait of William Penn the founder of the Province of Pennsylvania, from a Victorian book dated 1883 that is no longer in copyright," https://www.123rf.com/photo_17900109_an-engraved-vintage-illustration-portrait-of-william-penn-the-founder-of-the-province-of-pennsylvani.html.

Page 10: Matthew Merian (der Ältere), *Topographia Palatinatus Rheni...*, Frankfurt am Main, 1645, Section 8, 84-85, https://books.google.com.py/books?id=c2GaQgAACAAJ.

Page 12: Map created by Boyce Rensberger.

Page 15: Linda Lee Graham, "What's Lurking in Your Family Tree?" *Life in the 18ᵗʰ Century* (blog),n.d., http://www.lindaleegraham.com/whats-lurking-family-tree/.

Page 21: Courtesy Enoch Pratt Free Library.

Page 23: "A History of Road Building in Maryland," Report of the State Roads Commission, Operating Report for the Fiscal Years 1957-1958, (Baltimore, December 1958), 11, https://archive.org/details/reportofstateroa1957mary/page/11.

Page 31: Adapted from Grace L. Tracey and John P. Dern, *Pioneers of Old Monocacy: The Early Settlement of Frederick County, Maryland, 1721-1743* (Baltimore: Genealogical Publishing Co., Inc., 1987), 259.

Page 39: Frederick County Court Land Records, 1748-1752, B/270, MSA CE 108-1.

Page 43: William Cullen Bryand and Sydney Howard Gay, *A popular history of the United States*, vol. 3 (New York: Scribner, Armstrong and Company, 1876), 259, https://archive.org/details/popularhistoryofv3brya/page/n14.

Page 47: George Peck, D.D., *Wyoming: Its History, Stirring Incidents, and Romantic Adventures* (New York: Harper & Brothers, 1858), 241, https://archive.org/details/wyomingitshisto00peckgoog/page/n7.

Page 54: *Maryland Gazette*, Sept 5, 1765,1, MSA SC 2731, M 1280.

Page 58 and Chapter 10-various: H. L. Fischer, *'S Alt Marik-Haus Mittes In D'r Schtadt, Un Die Alte' Zeite*, illustr. by Henry Barratt (York: The York Republican, 1879).

Page 71: Reproduction of Lewis Miller image, Vol. 2, page 47, from the Collection of the York County Heritage Trust, York, PA. Used with permission.

Page 76: *Manual of Flax Culture, Seven Prize Essays, on the Culture of the Crop and the Dressing of the Fibre;* (New York: Orange Judd,

Agricultural Book Publisher, 1865), 6, https://hdl.handle.net/2027/hvd.hn3s98.

Pages cover, 105, 113-114, 116-117, 119-122, 124, 126-127, 130-131, 133-134: Photo credit: Boyce Rensberger. Courtesy of the Frederick County Landmarks Foundation.

Page 109: Courtesy of the Frederick County Landmarks Foundation.

Page 110: Drawing adapted from John D. Milner, AIA, *Schiefferstadt: A Restoration Study*, with contributions by Allan H. Steenhusen, Jeffrey C. Bourke and Alice Kent Schooler (West Chester: National Heritage Corporation, 1974), prepared for Frederick County Landmarks Foundation, Incorporated, illustration 3. Courtesy of the Frederick County Landmarks Foundation.

Page 111: Drawing adapted from Milner, *Schiefferstadt: A Restoration Study*, illustration 10. Courtesy of the Frederick County Landmarks Foundation.

Page 136: Photo credit: *Carl Brown Collection (MR4)*, Maryland Room, C. Burr Artz Public Library, Frederick County Public Libraries. On reverse of original photo is written: "Krantz farm house on Rosemont Ave. View from Frederick bypass—October, 1963."

APPENDIX 1
LAST WILL AND TESTAMENT OF ELIAS BRUNNER

In The Name of God Amen I Elias Brunner of Frederick County in the State of Maryland being thro the abundant Mercy and Goodness of God tho Weak in body Yet of a Sound and perfect understanding and Memory do constitute this my last Will and Testament and desire it may be received by all as Such—Imprimis I most Humbly bequeath my soul to God my maker beseeching his most gracious Acceptance of it through the all Sufficient Merits and Mediation of my most Compassionate Redeemer Jesus Christ who gave himself to be an Attonement for my Sins and is able to Save to the Uttermost all that come unto God by him seeing he ever liveth to make Intercession for them and who I trust will not reject me a returning penitent Sinner when I come to him for Mercy. In this Hope and Confidence I render up my Soul with Comfort humbly beseeching the most Blesses and Glorious Trinity One God most Holy most merciful and Gracious to prepare me for the time of my Dissolution and then to take me to himself into that peace and Rest and Incomparable Felicity which he has prepared (for)

[folio 8] for all that love and fear his Holy Name Amen—Blessed be God Imprimis I Give my Body to the Earth from whence it was Taken in full Assurance of its Resurrection from thence at the last Day to be Buried in a Christian like and Decent manner at the Discretion of my Executrix which is my Dear Wife Alberdina who I doubt not will manage it with all requesite Prudence—
Item I give to my Dear and loving Wife for Term of life this House and Lott whereon I now Dwell with all the Furniture about it and after her Death to my Son Peter Brunner, and after his Death to his Lawfull heirs and Assigns forever.

167

And as for my son Stephen Brunner he has had of me to the Value of Six hundred and Twenty pounds in cash in lieu of the said House and Lott above mentioned~

And after my Wifes Decease the whole personal Estate is to be Equally Divided between my two Sons Stephen and Peter—And I do hereby Constitute and Appoint my Dear and Beloved wife Alberdina my Sole Executrix of this my last Will and Testament Ratifying and Confirming this to be my last Will and Testament In Witness whereof I have hereunto set my hand and Seal the fourth day of August in the Year of our Lord Seventeen hundred and Eighty three—

Sealed Published and Declared
by the above named Elias Brunner
for and as his last will & Testament
Elias Brunner (signature)
in the presence of us & in the
presence of each other—
George Burckhartt
Conrad Doll
A McDonald

Frederick Town October 14, 1783   Then came Alberdina Brunner and made Oath on the Holy Evangelists of Almighty God (that)

[folio 9] that the foregoing Instrument of Writing is the True and whole Will and Testament of Elias Brunner late of Frederick County Deceased that have come to her hands and Possession and that she doth not known of an other—

G^{eo} Murdock Reg^r

Frederick Town October 14th 1783   Then came George Burkett Conrad Doll and Alexander McDonald the three Subscribing—Witnesses to the aforegoing last Will and Testament of Elias Brunner late of Frederick County Deceased and Severally made Oath on the Holy Evangelists of Almighty God that they did see the Testator therein named Sign and Seal this Will that they heard him Publish Pronounce and Declare the same to be his Last Will and Testament that at the time of his so doing he was to the best of their Apprehensions of sound and Disposing mind memory and understanding that they respectively Subscribed their names as Witnesses to this Will in the Presence and at the request of the Testator and in the Presence of each other—

G^eo Murdock Reg^r

On the 17th day of November 1783 came Alberdina Brunner the Widow of Elias Brunner late of Frederick County Deceased and made her Election to Stand to and Abide by the several legacies Bequeathed to her in the Will of her said Husband Deceased with regard to the real Estate and that she Claims her Dower or third part of the personal Estate according to Law

G^eo Murdock Reg^r

Frederick County Government
Register of Wills Frederick County, Maryland
Liber GM/No. 2/folio 7
October 14, 1783

Transcribed by P. Ogden
February 5, 2019

APPENDIX 2
INVENTORY OF ELIAS BRUNNER

During the colonial period in Maryland, a careful inventory was made of the personal effects found on the property of deceased heads of households. "Two court-appointed fellow citizens were charged with taking a 'true and perfect inventory of the goods, chattels and possessions' of a deceased citizen." To provide a value for the estate, appraisers assigned a monetary value to each item "to satisfy creditors and comply with the terms of a will." These documents are valuable to historians and descendants alike, for they give a glimpse into the material culture of previous generations. [*]

Inventory of Goods and Chattles belonging to the Estate of Elias Bruner deceased

Appraised by Conrad Grosch and George Burckhartt this 17th Nov 1783 ~ viz

	£	S	p
1 Cow 90/ 1 Still and furniture 180/	13	10	0
1 Cutting box and knife 15/ 2 saws and other lumber 15/	1	10	0
1 Hatchet 2 Hand Saws 1 Auger 1 drawing knife 1 Ax	1	2	6
6 Casks 20/ 7 Tubs 22/6 1 Churn 5/ 4 Cow Chains 12/	2	19	6
8 lb Hops 8/6 5 Pails 8/ 3 Iron Potts 30/ Earthenpotts 4/9	2	11	3
22 lb old pewter 27/6 Kitchen Lumber 22/6 Pott Rack and Cow Chain 12/6	3	2	6
1 Copper Kettle 40/ 1 Coffee Mill 7/6 4 Flat Irons 8/	2	15	6
1 qt Cann 4/ 1 pr Steelyards and 1 pair Scales 22/6	1	6	6
2 BedSteads 40/2 2 Feather Beds 200/	12	0	0
2 pr Curtains 70/ 4 Sheets 40/ 1 Cover for a Bed and Wallet 10/	6	0	0
1 Small Trunk 10/ 4 Cupboards 200/ 1 Clock 200/	20	10	0
1 Watch 90/ 3 Iron Stoves 300 2 Hogs 60/	22	10	0
3 Looking Glasses and 3 Spinning Wheels	2	10	0
5 Tables 13 Chairs and 7 Books	7	5	0
10 Bags 20/ 60 yards Hemp Linnen 120/	7	0	0
24 Yards Tow Linnen 30/ 1 Trunk 5/	2	3	0
1 Cradle 2 Heckles 32/6 1 Grind Stone 3/9	1	16	3
1 Grubing hoe 2 Scythes & a flour Chest	0	16	0
	£ 111	8	0

Conrad Grosh G[eo] Burckhart } App.[rs]
Stephen Bruner, Peter Brunner } Kin

Frederick County Novr 21st 1783

Then came Alberdina Bruner Executrix of Elias Bruner Late of Frederick County, Deceased, and made Oath on the Holy Evangels of Almighty God, that the aforegoing is a true and perfect Inventory of all and Singular the Goods and Chattles of the said deceased that hath come to her hands and Possession at the time of the making, that what hath Since or shall hereafter Come to her Hands & Possession she will Return in an additional Inventory, that she Knows of no Concealment of any part or parcel of the Decease d's Estate by any person whatsoever, and if she shall hereafter discover any Concealment or Suspect any to be, She will acquaint the Orphans Court with Such Concealment or Cause of Suspicion that it may be Enquired into according to Law.

(5 ½ Sides)   Geo. Murdoch Reg^r

Register of Wills, Frederick County, Maryland
Liber GM/No. 1/folio 476
November 21, 1783

Transcribed by P. Ogden
February 5, 2019

Elias Brunner sold the farm named Schifferstadt to Christopher Meyer in 1771 and moved to a residence in the City of Frederick Town. The items on this inventory, therefore, do not relate to Elias' residency at Schifferstadt.

*A very good monograph on colonial inventories can be found in the Maryland Historical Magazine of December, 1963. Titled "The Value of Personal Estates in Maryland, 1700-1710," it can be found on the website of the Maryland Historical Society: http://mdhs.msa.maryland.gov/pages/Login.aspx.

RESOURCES

Sources Available on the Internet

Many sources cited in this work are readily available to view on the internet. The reader will gain a deeper understanding of the information presented by accessing these sources.

Maryland Land Records –MDLandRec.net https://mdlandrec.net/main/index.cfm
Initially, this website requires the user to submit a request for a password before access will be granted. At the Welcome page, choose "County" to begin the search. Keep in mind that deeds dated prior to 1748 will be found in Prince George's County land records. Entering the clerk's initials (if applicable), book (liber) and page number (folio) as shown in each note will locate the cited document.

Maryland State Archives – Archives of Maryland Online (*AOMOL*) https://msa.maryland.gov/megafile/msa/speccol/sc2900/sc2908/html/volumes.html
On the "All Volumes" main page, entering the volume and page numbers, shown in each note, at the top of the page will display a full transcription of the document cited. Some original documents in this work were viewed in archival records at the Maryland State Archives, Hall of Records in Annapolis, Maryland, and are not available to view online.

FamilySearch -https://www.familysearch.org/
An email address is required to view the records here. This site contains

records held by the Mormon church. Wills, inventories and census records can be viewed on this site.

Maryland Historical Magazine - http://mdhs.msa.maryland.gov/pages/login.aspx
An email address is required to view issues of this magazine. A publication of the Maryland Historical Society, articles in this magazine have been a great source of accurate information for this book. Use the season and year listed in the endnote to find specific issues.

Other Source Information

The insurance policy cited in this work refers to a transcription of an original document, the first entry on which is dated 1848. Valuable descriptions of Schifferstadt and related buildings are contained in this document. A copy of this transcription is included in the archaeological survey conducted by ACS Consultants in 1995, *"History and Archaeology at the Schifferstadt Site (18FR134)*,*"* by Hettie Ballweber, which is available to view in the Maryland Room, C. Burr Artz Public Library, Frederick County Public Libraries, Frederick, MD.

A detailed architectural survey report, "Schiefferstadt: a restoration study," prepared for Frederick County Landmarks Foundation by National Heritage Corporation, 1974," is available for patrons to view in the Research Center at Heritage Frederick.

INDEX